Praise for
Guns, An American Conversation

"The team at Spaceship Media has produced the clearest and most inspiring guide to civil discourse I've seen to date. This is so much more than a book about guns. This is a soul-nourishing and provocative vision of a world in which conversation, community, and technology can bring us closer together instead of farther apart—and one that provides us all with the tools we need to get there. Ultimately, through the stories of others, *Guns, An American Conversation* reminds us of our own potential for decency and humanity. If a small team of journalists and a moderated Facebook group can build genuine community and nuanced conversation around the ever-divisive issue of guns, you just might be able to have a thoughtful conversation with your crazy uncle at Thanksgiving."

—Lisa Conn, cofounder and COO of Icebreaker,
an online community events organization

"How do we find 'we the people' in our polarized nation? *Guns, An American Conversation* offers a road map using dialogue and journalism to tackle complex, conflicted issues. By connecting with curiosity and compassion, people discover their shared humanity. Try it."

—Peggy Holman, cofounder of Journalism That Matters,
author of *Engaging Emergence: Turning Upheaval into Opportunity*, and coauthor of *The Change Handbook*

"This book isn't just about guns. It's about learning to live in the same world with other people."

—Laurie L. Putnam, San Jose State University

"*Guns, An American Conversation* offers a rare bit of hope in this polarized time that Americans are still capable of upholding the fragile core values that underpin our democratic experiment in self-governance: to deliberate over matters of public interest, consider other points of view, and make well-informed choices.

"This book offers practical guidance and a host of resources for news organizations seeking to experiment with dialogue journalism, including clear steps to follow to facilitate productive conversations and many lively examples of how debate can play out in a constructive if impassioned way. The point is not to change minds, necessarily, but to open space for listening to one another and to ensure that arguments have a factual basis. Many have long espoused these goals, but Spaceship Media is taking concrete steps toward making them happen, and what they have learned will be useful as this country continues to wrestle with many painful divides."

—Carrie Brown, social journalism director,
Craig Newmark Graduate School of Journalism at CUNY

"The real-world efforts in this book show that people experiencing facts together in the context of dialogue and respectful disagreement reach greater understanding than those who just pelt facts *at* people. Equally, *Guns* inspires readers to, at the most defensive of moments, slow down, reinvigorate their curiosity about others' perspectives, and measure their own words carefully. It's a new way to rebuild democratic communities in a multicultural America."

—Subbu Vincent, director of journalism and media ethics,
Markkula Center for Applied Ethics,
Santa Clara University

"This book offers a timely case study in the practice of dialogue journalism—an innovative model that uses journalism to support nuanced conversations on polarizing issues. As it unpacks the complexity of the gun debate in the US, it offers valuable insights on a process that should be of interest to journalists, journalism educators and students, and anyone working to bridge divides."

—Andrea Wenzel, PhD, author of *Community-Centered Journalism: Engaging People, Exploring Solutions, and Building Trust*

"*Guns, An American Conversation* shows that not only are complicated and nuanced conversations possible in the midst of what seems like never-ending turmoil and tribalism, they are necessary if we have any genuine intention to make progress in collaborating toward solutions. The work of Spaceship Media is a clear and accessible road map to putting dialogue journalism into practice across the spectrum of difficult conversations we all need to be having."

—Heather Bryant, founder of Project Facet

"This engaging book is both a close-up exploration of Americans' complex beliefs about guns and a handbook for how journalism can engage deeply to bring citizens together across differences. 'Dialogue journalism' offers journalists a path toward a more meaningful public-service role and deepens the civic bonds on which democracy depends. In a time of unprecedented challenges for journalism and society, *Guns, An American Conversation* offers hope for both."

—Regina Lawrence, associate dean,
School of Journalism and Communication,
University of Oregon

"Too much of what passes for engagement in American journalism puts journalists at the center of the work. Spaceship Media's model is different. Instead of encouraging the public to help journalists do their jobs, dialogue journalism asks journalists to help the citizenry do its job—by making space for honest, informed, and empathetic conversations among people who profoundly disagree on matters of civic importance like gun violence. It's a model that, allowed to scale, could create the social capital and trust in media necessary for democracy to thrive."

—Linda Miller, board member, Journalism That Matters

GUNS

An American Conversation

How to Bridge Political Divides

The Editors at SPACESHIP MEDIA

TILLER PRESS

New York   London   Toronto   Sydney   New Delhi

TILLER PRESS

An Imprint of Simon & Schuster, Inc.
1230 Avenue of the Americas
New York, NY 10020

First Tiller Press hardcover edition September 2020

TILLER PRESS and colophon are trademarks of Simon & Schuster, Inc.

For information about special discounts for bulk purchases, please
contact Simon & Schuster Special Sales at 1-866-506-1949
or business@simonandschuster.com.

The Simon & Schuster Speakers Bureau can bring authors to your live event.
For more information or to book an event, contact the Simon & Schuster Speakers
Bureau at 1-866-248-3049 or visit our website at www.simonspeakers.com.

Interior design by Laura Levatino

Manufactured in the United States of America

1   3   5   7   9   10   8   6   4   2

Library of Congress Cataloging-in-Publication Data

Names: Spaceship Media (Organization), author.
Title: Guns, an American conversation : how to bridge political divides /
by Spaceship Media.
Description: First Tiller Press hardcover edition. | New York : Tiller Press, 2020. |
Includes bibliographical references and index.
Identifiers: LCCN 2020016767 (print) | LCCN 2020016768 (ebook) |
ISBN 9781982132989 (hardcover) | ISBN 9781982132996 (ebook)
Subjects: LCSH: Gun control—United States. | Firearms ownership—United States.
Classification: LCC HV7436 .S63 2020 (print) | LCC HV7436 (ebook) |
DDC 363.330973—dc23
LC record available at https://lccn.loc.gov/2020016767
LC ebook record available at https://lccn.loc.gov/2020016768

ISBN 978-1-9821-3298-9
ISBN 978-1-9821-3299-6 (ebook)

Contents

Contents

Foreword

Spaceship Media launched after the 2016 election with a mission to reduce polarization, restore trust in journalism, and build communities. A longtime journalist, I was disheartened and distressed as I watched the rising vitriol and nastiness in our public spaces, both online and off. So I decided to do something new. I wanted to go to the heart of divides, as journalists always have. But instead of writing stories, quoting practiced, partisan voices on each side, in a frame that can sometimes inadvertently amplify divides, I instead wanted to see if I could engage regular Americans in substantive, fact-based conversations about the divisive issues that shape our society.

Since its inception, Spaceship Media has created conversations about polarizing issues such as immigration, policing, race, education, and the environment. We used our novel approach, what we call dialogue journalism, to help convene

Foreword

"Guns, An American Conversation," which brought twenty-one people with a wide range of views from across the nation. They gathered in Washington, DC, for a weekend in April 2018 to discuss their opinions, values, and ideas. Afterward they joined 130 others in a monthlong, moderated conversation on Facebook.

In the conversations that Spaceship Media hosts, we invite people to shed their reflexive anger and rehearsed talking points. We want to help participants do the hard work of slowing down enough to tease out nuance, to make space for curiosity, to understand one another's views and values. We invite people to see one another as multifaceted people, not as caricatures of particular political positions or views. We invite them to engage as the complex people they are. We support those conversations with reporting.

While ours is a new approach to journalism—you'll read all about how the process unfolds in this book—journalism has historically played a role in supporting the public square, in bolstering the reasoned exchange of ideas and views. Consider letters to the editors, opinion columns, and editorials. Consider the reporting, deep or daily, that people have relied on to discuss the issues that matter to real people in cities and towns across the nation. Journalism is at the heart of how we get our information, how we engage with ideas, and ultimately how we engage with the larger community. But this ultradivided moment in our nation calls for new responses. It calls for more active, intentional approaches to serving communities.

At Spaceship Media, to help rebuild trust with the communities we serve, we invite journalists to lead with their authenticity; to remember, in the broadest sense, that we are all in this together. And we invite the participants of our conversations to engage with the same mind-set. The path forward out of the current political and social state of affairs requires resisting the reflex to vilify and stereotype one another. Not all gun owners are the same, nor are all gun control activists the same (nor are all journalists the same). We all come to our beliefs and views through our own experiences. Let us be human together; then we can talk.

In doing this work, I often hear, "Why should I talk to them?" People tell me that "they" (those with whom they disagree) are crazy, evil, mean, or difficult. They say "I feel attacked." But we are talking about neighbors talking—and, especially, listening—to neighbors, family, students. And in cases of divisive issues, talking makes more sense than going to war.

The challenges journalists face—not to amplify divides, not to race to the shiny objects, tragedies, and celebrities—are not so different from those we all face as humans. Let's not forget, we as humans are the ones who click on divisive content. We are the ones who post mocking memes, who name-call with playful vigor, who retweet and repost. The challenge is how do we, both as journalists and as citizens, put kindness and respect first? Journalism's reckoning is a human reckoning.

Through this book's window into one of the United States's most divisive issues, you'll see how regular people and journalists alike wrestle with how to engage across lines about guns and gun safety. My hope is that you will see it as a window into possibility, that it will help you remember that despite what pundits and polls might have us believe, the vast majority of us have views that are more nuanced than not, less extreme than not. And, perhaps most importantly, the vast majority of us want more or less the same things: to be able to live safe, happy, and productive lives.

I am wildly grateful to the conversation of participants from across the country who opened their hearts and minds to be a part of this project. I am deeply indebted to the journalists and leadership from our partners at Advance Digital who worked so determinedly and creatively to build something that mattered in the months following the Parkland shooting. They also took a great leap of courage by financing this project and marshaling their resources from across the country to make it manifest.

So please enjoy this look into our experiment in a journalism-supported conversation about guns. I hope it inspires you to listen to others in ways that can help us at least begin to understand different perspectives and ideas about the challenging issues that shape our society. Because, after all, it is our society to make and keep, to have and to hold.

Eve Pearlman,
cofounder of Spaceship Media

GUNS
An American Conversation

Chapter 1

It's not that school shootings were uncommon before February 13, 2018. But when fourteen students and three staff members were killed at Marjory Stoneman Douglas High School in Parkland, Florida, that day, it was close to two decades since two teens at Columbine High School in Colorado shot and killed a teacher and twelve fellow students, in April 1999. And, again, the nation was cast into a moment of regret, reckoning, and turmoil.

These moments, like so many before, pass through our nation's news cycle quickly. At first there's a chorus of angry voices all around: battered, gridlocked, dysfunctional. Story piles on story, tweet on tweet, Facebook post on Facebook post, nearly all reactive, explosive, polarized. Journalists cover the stories in a grief-filled us-vs.-them, good-guy-vs.-bad-guy narrative— and then the cycle repeats itself with another shooting.

Yet soon after the Parkland shooting, in an emerging form of journalism, a black man in Colorado passionately explained what he saw as a need to legally carry firearms, and to teach others how to use them, amid racist assumptions that black men who dress a certain way are dangerous—and therefore more likely to be assailed themselves. His reality, right or wrong for others, had never been fully thought through by those in this particular dialogue.

In the same new-journalism online discussion, a Louisiana attorney articulated how the AR-15 assault-style rifle, a weapon linked to a number of mass shootings and to many Americans deserving of banishment, is versatile and can be used for lawful hunting, target practice, or self-protection. As described by gun enthusiasts, an AR-15 for a skilled sports shooter is like a fast Porsche for a fast-car lover.

Others in the group were discussing whether schools should teach firearms training, since school shootings tend to involve students. A teacher from the Midwest replied, "We have enough to do [as teachers]. Every time there's a societal problem, our only answer is 'Teach it at school.' I am no more going to teach gun safety than I am going to teach you how to do your taxes or change a tire." (As for the fast-car AR-15 comparison, there was pushback from people who noted this country has speeding laws—to which the Louisiana attorney replied yes, but "driving fun is not based on a constitutionally protected right.")[1]

None of this has stopped a shooting or necessarily changed anyone's mind. But it was a new and different kind of conversation, guided by journalists and professionals who wanted to support people on opposite sides in talking to one another—without judgment, and with the goal of seeing if both sides on contentious issues can begin to understand what drives the other. Longtime journalists Eve Pearlman and Jeremy Hay launched this new method of conversation through their organization Spaceship Media after the 2016 election, intent on bridging these pronounced divides, intent on inviting people to slow down, to listen openly, to lead with genuine curiosity, to shed their practiced partisan talking points. Pearlman and Hay created a methodology, what they call dialogue journalism, to support the dialogue that a functioning democracy requires.

"We want these conversations to extend empathy, to help us learn to see the humanity and validity of those with whom we disagree, to understand that their views and ideas come from their experiences and that they are not only those views, we are all whole people in this together," explained Pearlman.

To create these conversation projects, nourished by journalism, Spaceship Media partners with established news organizations. For "Guns, An American Conversation" they partnered with Advance Publications, the ninth-largest journalism organization in the country, which funded the project, and with Essential Partners, which designed and facilitated the two-day kickoff in DC.

Collaborating closely with Advance Local's editorial director, John Hassell, and Michelle Holmes, vice president of Alabama Media Group, an Advance property, they worked in tandem to create the conversation.[2]

Advance Local
and Alabama Media Group

Alabama Media Group operates AL.com, one of the country's largest local websites, producing television and video programming and publishing Alabama's three most prominent newspapers: the *Birmingham News*, the *Huntsville Times*, and the *Mobile Press-Register*. AMG's parent company, Advance Local, is a leading media company, with newspapers and websites across the country comprising twelve news and information websites and more than thirty affiliated newspapers.[3]

In Alabama, Holmes had built a newsroom primed for innovation, supporting projects and partnerships that pushed the boundaries of journalistic practice. Spaceship Media had worked with her team twice before, collaborating on "Talking Politics," a conversation between Trump supporters and Clinton supporters after the 2016 election. In the second, "Tackling the Gap," Spaceship Media brought educators together to talk about the racial achievement gap in Alabama's public schools.

Their third collaboration, conceived of in the days just after Parkland, would become "Guns, An American Conversation." Central to their aim: to use journalism to create and foster a nationwide, civil conversation about guns and gun safety.

For Spaceship Media, the goal of their work is not to change minds but rather to create spaces for respectful dialogue with the support of reporting, and to rebuild trust between people on opposite sides of polarizing issues and journalism.

"We think of building a triangle of trust," explained Pearlman. "Between divided communities and the journalists who serve them."

Spaceship Media's work hinges on the idea that by asking people to listen first, to listen carefully, to shed their practiced partisan talking points, to lead with curiosity, that we can begin to have the sorts of conversations that allow people with different ideologies to understand one another.

"At every stage of our work, we're as transparent as possible about our methods and our motives. At every stage, we take the time to answer people's questions—explain why we're doing what we're doing. We tell people that it's not a trap: no one's there to tell you you're stupid, no one's there to tell you your experience doesn't matter. And we always ask for a really different sort of behavior, a repatterning away from the reflexive name-calling so entrenched in our discourse that most of us, on all sides, don't even notice it anymore," explained Pearlman.

And that understanding makes a difference.

The conversation would begin in March 2018, with an in-person gathering of twenty-one people representing a broad range of views and beliefs and a team of journalists from Advance Local around the country at the Newseum in Washington, DC. Helping guide the potentially difficult human element that weekend—the work, conversations, and exercises needed for participants to interact, share personal and even painful stories with strangers in the room, to shed their psychological armor and suspend their judgments—was a team from Essential Partners, a nonprofit whose facilitators are skilled in communication and bridging differences.

Then, immediately after two days of discussions, those twenty-one people joined a larger monthlong, curated Facebook group, moderated and supported with reporting from Advance's team of journalists, but directed, in many ways, by the participants themselves.

Spaceship Media puts into practice a way for journalists to interact with divided communities. They use their skills to support civil, civic dialogue about difficult social and political issues. That work is guided by the principle that dialogue across differences is essential to a functioning democracy, and that it is the responsibility of journalism and journalists to play a multifaceted role in supporting these kinds of relationships.

The Seven Steps of Dialogue Journalism

1. The Build

We work with news organizations to identify communities that aren't talking or are in conflict and design a conversation experience through which they can engage constructively.

2. The Gather

We explore with each of these communities what they think of one another and what they would like to know about the other.

3. The Welcome

We bring the communities together in an environment designed to welcome people as individuals, not simply as avatars of a particular political, social, or cultural position.

4. The Experience

We support an experience that revolves around the participants as much as if not more than our aims or those of the sponsoring organizations; it is a rare opportunity to engage deeply with others with whom they disagree.

5. The Carry

We moderate our conversations closely, helping people engage respectfully with one another and using tested techniques to help create a productive experience.

6. The Nourish

As conversations grow, we support them with reporting and research that provide information to the participants, with the aim of establishing an agreed-upon foundation of facts for their discussions.

7. The Share

With newsroom partners, we uncover stories generated in the conversation, including ongoing questions and issues relevant to the community; this amplifies the conversation's impact and provides additional opportunities for engagement.[4]

Spaceship Media honed these steps in their first major project, "Talking Politics," which brought together fifty women: twenty-five Trump supporters from Alabama and twenty-five Clinton supporters from California.[5]

At the start of each monthlong moderated conversation, Spaceship Media invites participants on both sides to answer a series of questions, including "What do you think 'they' [the other side] thinks about you?" They do this to surface common stereotypes and judgments and to give people a chance to reflect on them.

"We find that people look at these negative assumptions, both their own and other people's, and immediately recognize their inaccuracy, which opens the door to more thoughtful, open dialogue," explained Pearlman.

The Trump supporters said things such as,

- "They think we are religious Bible thumpers."
- "That we're backward and hickish, and stupid."
- "They think that we all have Confederate flags in our yards, that we're racist and sexist and uneducated."

The Clinton supporters felt equally misjudged.

- "They think we're snobby and we're elitist."
- "We're godless and we're permissive with our children."
- "They think that we're elitist, pie-in-the-sky intellectuals, rich people, Whole Foods–eating, very out of touch."

The participants went on to have an experience that, for many of them, was meaningful and transformative.

Among the women in the group was Courtney Hall, an attorney and law professor from Alabama whose politics are deeply informed by her faith. She joined the group to dispel some of those stereotypes.

"One of the reasons I wanted to participate in the project," Hall said, "is because I felt a lot of Clinton voters dismissed Trump voters' positions as xenophobic, racist, and sexist." She continued, "I have a lot of respect for the Clinton voters in this group, and I feel that through this they have a respect for my position as well."[6]

One of the Clinton voters Hall was referring to was Brittany Walker Pettigrew. Right after the election, the California social worker was invited to be part of the cross-partisan, cross-state-lines conversation. At first she was reluctant to join.

She thought, *No way am I participating in that.*

But then she thought about her own very racially, ethnically, and politically diverse family. Maybe she had some insight that might be useful in this Facebook experiment. She knew that the stereotypical version of a Trump voter did not represent the Trump voters she knew personally.

"One of the things I took away from it was that over the years in my life, I never fully engaged people across differences because I was afraid of the consequences," said Walker Pettigrew. "But I came to see that there was very little risk. As a result I just started speaking."

The women in the group participated in deep, often uncomfortable, conversations around a variety of topics such as health care, reproductive rights, gun control, and how their views on these subjects affected their voting decisions. Spaceship Media began this dialogue, as they do each project, by asking the participants four questions meant to prompt self-reflection and openness before diving into conversation. They asked,

- What do you think about the other community?
- What do you think they think about you?
- What do you want to know about them?
- What do you want them to know about you?

From there, the Spaceship Media team periodically steered the discussions by creating posts and commenting in a Facebook group while also encouraging participants to create their own posts and conversations. Quickly the group took on a life of its own, with participants on both sides taking ownership of the group and independently starting and maintaining discussions. Notably, members spent some time experimenting with reading each other's news sources. Looking at where and how other people—especially people on opposite "sides"—get their news and information often helps deepen understanding of how others think and experience the news.

Because of her leadership as a participant in "Talking Politics," the "Guns" team invited Walker Pettigrew to join the team of moderators. Moderators serve as minders for the online conversation, prompting discussion, asking questions, and interjecting when things get heated. The moderators work together to support participants in the conversation in taking breaks when they get angry, reframing questions that come off as hostile or accusatory, and working to assume the best intentions of those they are talking to.[7]

Essential Partners, a decades-old nonprofit with experience hosting difficult conversations, was recruited to facilitate the project, not only for the in-person gathering in DC but also to support the journalists-moderators behind the scenes in the month that followed. Essential Partners relies on strategies developed by family therapists to promote effective communication in the midst of painful differences. They also incorporate insights and tools from mediation, psychology, and neurobiology. Their work enables people to share experiences and explore questions that both clarify their own perspectives and help them become more comfortable around, and curious about, those with whom they disagree.

• • •

To begin the project, the organizers selected a team of journalists from across the nine states where Advance Local has newsrooms to serve as moderators and reporters. The team worked in close cooperation with Spaceship Media and Essential Partners to host and support the in-person gathering of community members, which would be followed immediately by the monthlong, online discussion. The search for the participants began with an invitation to join the conversation posted in Advance's newspapers and on Advance's news sites across the country, including newsrooms in New Jersey, Massachusetts, Ohio, and Oregon.

More than a thousand people heeded the call to be a part of the project, answering questions in an online form designed to encourage reflection about their thoughts and feelings about guns and gun safety:

- What is your/your family's story about or relationship to guns?
- How have guns impacted you/your family?
- What do you want to know about those on the other side of the gun control debate?
- What do you want those on the other side of the gun control debate to know about you?

The journalists were looking for people with a wide range of views who were open to a respectful, fact-based conversation about guns and gun safety. People were of course deeply rooted in their own values, ideas, and beliefs, but they were also open to considering what others, on the other "side," thought and felt. An instant disqualifier? Saying in the opening questionnaire that they weren't interested in talking to those with whom they disagree.

The goal was not only a diversity of opinions, but also diversity in geography, gender, race, religion, and age. With the participant group identified, the collaborators invited twenty-one people to Washington, DC, for a weekend of talking, reflecting, and connecting. In preparation for the gathering, Advance reporters did some research, creating a detailed report about the one sentence of the amendment that often sits at the center of our national divide about guns and gun safety: *A well regulated Militia, being necessary to the security of a free State, the right of the people to keep and bear Arms, shall not be infringed.*

Such reports are part of Spaceship Media's process to help clarify topics and provide needed context during the conversations. Spaceship Media calls this style of reporting FactStacks, and they use these to provide participants with reporting and information so they can have a shared set of facts to undergird their discussions. In this project, Advance reporter Stephen Koff wrote a FactStack about the Second Amendment.

The Second Amendment and the Courts

What does the Second Amendment say?

"A well regulated Militia, being necessary to the security of a free State, the right of the people to keep and bear Arms, shall not be infringed."

How has the US Supreme Court interpreted that?

There have been two primary interpretations over the past eighty-two years. In 1938, the Supreme Court ruled in *United States v. Miller* that Congress could regulate a sawed-off shotgun that had moved in interstate commerce under the National Firearms Act of 1934 because the evidence did not suggest that the shotgun "has some reasonable relationship to the preservation or efficiency of a well regulated militia," according to Cornell Law School's Legal Information Institute. The court then explained "that the Framers included the Second Amendment to ensure the effectiveness of the military."[8]

Then in 2008, the high court ruled 5–4 that the right to firearms was an individual right, not just a collective one—that is, it is linked not only to a militia but also to "the inherent right of self defense." The court in this case, *District of Columbia v. Heller*, struck down the DC laws banning handguns and requiring other firearms to be disassembled and unloaded or bound by a trigger lock or similar device.[9]

"There seems to us no doubt, on the basis of both text and history, that the Second Amendment conferred an individual right to keep and bear arms," Justice Antonin Scalia wrote for the majority.

But he added that the Second Amendment right "is not unlimited."

"Although we do not undertake an exhaustive historical analysis today of the full scope of the Second Amendment, nothing in our opinion should be taken to cast doubt on longstanding prohibitions on the possession of firearms by felons and the mentally ill, or laws forbidding the carrying of firearms in sensitive places such as schools and government buildings, or laws imposing conditions and qualifications on the commercial sale of arms," Scalia wrote.

What was the impact of that ruling?

In a series of federal appeals since the *Heller* ruling, states and cities have won the right to uphold certain restrictions while losing the ability to ban firearms altogether. These cases have been argued not only on the basis of *Heller* but also on *McDonald v. Chicago*,[10] in which the Supreme Court said in a narrow 2010 ruling that Second Amendment right to firearms applied not only to the federal government (the District of Columbia is a federal city) but also to cities and states. Chicago and its suburb of Oak Park had contended that their restrictions effectively banning most handguns were constitutional because the Second Amendment had no application to states.

The Supreme Court disagreed in a 5–4 opinion, saying that self-defense is a basic right. But the ruling, written by Justice Samuel Alito, added that the exceptions allowed in *Heller*—that the Second Amendment does not confer a limitless right—would also apply to states: "Despite municipal respondents' doomsday proclamations, incorporation does not imperil every law regulating firearms."

What were cases that followed?

The Fifth US Circuit Court of Appeals cited *Heller* in 2013[11] when it said that Texas had the right to disallow people under ages eighteen, nineteen, and twenty from carrying handguns in public. The Texas law adhered to "Texas's stated goal of maintaining public safety" while still allowing "18–20-year-olds to have handguns in their cars and homes and to apply for concealed handgun licenses as soon as they turn 21," the appeals court said in *National Rifle Association v. McCraw*.[12]

A different court, the Ninth US Circuit Court of Appeals, similarly used the rationale of *Heller* in 2014 when it said that San Francisco had the right to require handguns be stored and locked when not on the person of an adult. The city's trigger lock requirement "is substantially related to the important government interest of reducing firearm-related deaths and injuries," the Ninth Circuit Court said.[13]

While this created a burden seemingly at odds with the Second Amendment, the court said, the San Francisco ordinance differed from the District of Columbia's attempt at a broader ban because it did "not substantially prevent law-abiding citizens from using firearms to defend themselves in the home."

**What about attempts to restrict
guns that fire rounds rapidly,
loosely known as assault weapons?**

The *Washington Post* reported that there have been four such cases challenging states' so-called assault weapons ban in federal appeals courts since the Supreme Court's *Heller* decision. "In each case that has reached a federal appeals court since then, bans on the semiautomatic guns known as assault weapons have been upheld, usually for the same two reasons," the *Post* said in late February of 2018.[14] "Banning them, the courts have said, does not curtail the right of self-defense protected by the Constitution. There are plenty of other weapons—handguns and regular long guns—available to people to protect themselves. At the same time, the courts have said, states and municipalities have legitimate reasons to ban AR-15-style weapons because of the dangers they pose, to schools, innocent bystanders and police."[15]

With the big-picture basics laid out, the journalists and participants gathered in Washington, DC, over a March weekend. They were there to learn about careful, attentive listening against the backdrop of protests outside. Crowds were taking to the streets as part of the nationwide March for Our Lives, a movement catalyzed by survivors of the Parkland shooting.[16]

Crowds of people streamed through the streets outside the Newseum in downtown DC, where the participants and journalists of the project had come together. Outside picture windows, a slow-moving human river with signs bobbed along with slogans such as,

- "Guns Don't Die, Children Do."
- "Never Again."
- "We Call Bullsh*t."

The atmosphere outside was a mixture of grief and fury. A roster of Parkland students advocated for an end to gun violence. Emma González, a Parkland survivor, had the crowd repeat the names of the students who were killed, then stood in silence, tears streaming down her face.[17] When she spoke she explained that her six minutes and twenty seconds onstage was the same amount of time it took for the shooter to complete his killing spree, ending the lives of her friends.[18]

There were similar actions at eight hundred locations across the country and around the world. Scattered counterprotests were held simultaneously by groups who support Second Amendment rights.

Wayne LaPierre, the head of the National Rifle Association, weighed in a few days after Parkland, presenting the position of the powerful lobbying group during a speech at the Conservative Political Action Conference in Oxon Hill, Maryland.[19]

Armed security is the only way to stop school shootings, LaPierre said. Schools are soft targets that need to be hardened. Guns are not the cause of death and pain. "Evil walks among us," he said. "And God help us if we don't harden our schools and protect our kids."

It was amid this state of heightened discord that the small group of journalists and community members began their meeting inside the Newseum.

Like the streets outside, the room inside the Newseum represented a diversity of voices, opinions, age, geography, and background. In addition to the twenty-one participants from across the country, several organizers from Advance Local, Essential Partners, and Spaceship Media would be taking part in the two-day discussion.

Essential Partners' John Sarrouf welcomed everyone and set the tone for the group's introductions with some thoughtful instruction: "The first thing that people should do is turn to each other and say 'tell me a story to help me understand how you've come to the beliefs that you have about guns.' Then we should get into values. What values do you hold that you really care about that lead you to think the way you do? Where is this complex for you, because so often when we're in conflict with other people, we get flat. You're just progun, I'm just antigun, or I'm just pro this, you're just that. But none of us are just one thing. All of us are more complex, so ask about the complexity and share your own."[20]

And so the introductions began, opening doors to dialogue and connection. Every one of the participants with a different story, every one acknowledging the importance of dialogue and productive conversation.

• • •

Despite all the hubbub and noise outside, the group created a sense of quiet community.

The personal stories nestled in those introductions created a climate of humanity and human connection that would be the foundation as the conversation moved forward, a touchstone to recall when fatigue set in and tempers flared later in the project.

Private moments that first day helped. As the journalists left the room to discuss and further plan their roles, which would be played out in newsrooms and offices from New York to California, John Sarrouf and Parisa Parsa, both from Essential Partners, closed the door and kept the group of participants behind. What they discussed has never been entirely public, nor does it need to be. But in a space intended to be safe and free of judgment, some shared personal stories involving safety, fear, pride, violence, family suicide, and school threats, the deep-seated issues through which beliefs and values are shaped, held, and defended.

That individual recognition is missing in the American conversation, and understanding the power of such moments is part of what's missing across traditional journalism. "There's a huge gap between how we understand other people and how we feel understood by them," said Sarrouf.[21]

That's what "Guns, An American Conversation" hoped to change. Understanding, empathy—that's what is at the core of dialogue journalism.

Chapter 2

The conversations that Spaceship Media hosts are designed to be open and honest, but that doesn't mean they aren't challenging and rich with opinion. "This is not about tea and crumpets," as Spaceship Media cofounder Jeremy Hay likes to say. The conversation organizers work to create an environment and structure to support people in engaging productively on difficult issues.

"For us, a core belief is that when given guidance and support in doing so, many of us can and will talk respectfully and substantively about the issues that divide us," said Pearlman. For "Guns, An American Conversation" Spaceship Media created a detailed plan, or "rules on engagement," for the participants.

Rules of the Conversation

First, we are very grateful to you for your willingness to participate in one of the nation's most important conversations. The debate over the issue of guns is rarely civil and often simply devolves to shouting or disengagement. We believe you will help demonstrate that Americans can do it differently, that we can discuss these issues productively and perhaps find some common ground—with thoughtfulness and civility despite our often dramatic differences in opinion and position. That said, this is not a debate; it is not about winning. It is about demonstrating that we can have civil conversations with people who disagree with us about these vital issues. Please enter it in that spirit.

This project and our work are guided by the principle that our democracy suffers if we can't talk to one another across our differences, if we can't learn to understand and respect our varied beliefs, experiences, and ideas. Your participation here supports the country we share.

On to the details:

"Guns, An American Conversation" takes place in a closed, moderated Facebook group.

Only people invited into the group can see and take part in the conversations.

The group will be moderated by at least five people; they will introduce themselves in the group. Their (and our) role is to support you in having as meaningful, productive, and valuable an experience as possible.

There is no requirement for participation. Post and comment as much or as little as you want! Think and observe as you'd like, and jump in as you'd like.

Advance Local is a news organization. *Time* magazine is also documenting this process. So don't be surprised if we reach out to you with an interview request. You can always say no. And you will never be quoted without your explicit permission, nor will your Facebook comments be used without your permission.

As discussion arises in the group about different topics, we will have reporters available to research those topics and provide information back to the group to inform the discussions. Please feel free to ask for information and to share questions and concerns with us about that process.

Ask questions! Share stories of your life! Explain your thinking. The more you can tap into your curiosity to make this meaningful—and the less you try to win the argument or change someone else's mind—the more productive an experience it will probably be.

A few rules: please don't post GIFs or memes—you know, the little pictures with often-times sarcastic sayings. They often just stop conversations instead of leading them forward.

Also, if you post an article, please explain why it appealed to you, what you learned from it, or what it made you think about it. Use it to prompt a discussion or even ask a specific question.

Please think about how the words you use will sound and feel to people with different viewpoints from you. The conversation isn't a place to score political points—it's a place to learn about how other people think and what they value and, in the process, maybe learn more about what you think and value.

No name calling! This includes people in the group as well as those out of it; this includes politicians, groups, ideas. Calling someone's candidate a name is essentially calling that someone a name. Name calling is so embedded in our political conversations right now that sometimes it's even hard to notice we're doing

> it—if you think you might be, take a moment and think before you post.
>
> There are plenty of places we can all go on the internet to exchange barbs and quips, to play I gotcha, and to fight to win. This is not that internet :) Please join us in a place to listen, learn, think, understand.
>
> If there is a place in the conversation you'd like to bring to the attention of the moderators— we're here to help.[1]

The moderators received training and guidance in the role that would call on them to walk careful lines between structuring the conversation and letting it flow freely. The role of moderator would be far from easy, as it would require paying close attention to the participants' needs, maintaining a policy of listening first, and ultimately working to support the best nature of the participants. The moderators would be the ones responsible for holding the conversation together and maintaining its structure.[2] To help them in this difficult role, Spaceship Media provided guidelines:

> Over here at Spaceship Media, we think of moderation as having something in common with teaching. We set high expectations; we

help people rise to their best; we ignore mild negative behavior; we highlight (by engaging, liking, and commenting on) positive behavior; wc know that people perform better when they feel loved and respected, so we offer our love and respect. We are relentlessly positive. We see our role as moderators as helping people have a rewarding experience.

- **Letting Them Know We're Paying Attention:** Drop in on threads, make a comment, "like" something; in other words, let the participants know that you are around—so you can be called on for help if necessary and so they are mindful of how they act.

- **Whole Person/Diversion:** No one wants to talk about race and the achievement gap all the time; most people need a break and want to be known for more than just their opinions and views. Ask about their weekend plans, favorite recipes, or favorite reading, whatever. More importantly, encourage participants to engage with each other about "off-center" subjects so that where possible they build some form of relationship off the topic.

- **Sideline Conversation** (one-on-one via Messenger or other means): When you see comment threads getting heated, or running into a wall (or seeming to be headed that way), consider checking in with the conversants individually. Ask how they are, acknowledge that they are engaged in something difficult, and ask how you can help. This is akin to letting them know you are there, but it is more: it is engaging with someone personally to reinforce their belief that they can stay the course of a challenging path. Empathize with them— meaning, recognize what they're experiencing without siding with one against another. Remember, you don't want to disparage or malign the other "side." But that doesn't mean you can't recognize that these topics are hard and charged. An opportunity to vent, recognition that they are trying hard, and a suggestion to take a break if they need to can help people.[3]

During the life of the project, moderators had frequent conversations among themselves about how to handle specific issues, how to juggle strong personalities, and when either moderators or participants needed to vent or step away from the group when things got too intense. They would work around the clock in scheduled shifts of a few hours, monitoring the participants, approving posts at set times, and skillfully guiding the conversation, collectively recording all of their notes on a master document. In addition to posting directly in the group, moderators had the ability to connect with individual participants via Facebook Messenger, email, or phone call. In addition to their training from Spaceship Media, the moderators joined a messenger chat to collaborate on how and when to respond most effectively to points of difficulty and strife within the conversation. Realizing the importance of the project, the moderators were equally excited and anxious to start.

And with ground rules and guidelines established for participants as well as moderators and reporters, the conversation officially began on April 4, 2018.

To set the tone for the monthlong Facebook conversation, lead moderator Enrique Lavin kicked off the group by posting a picture of himself smiling while ice fishing on water that looked a little too liquid for safety. That Lavin posted such a personal photo reflects Spaceship Media's approach to conducting this type of difficult conversation. People tend to tire quickly if they are constantly discussing difficult issues. Keeping that in mind, in its conversations, the team looked to mix the light with the heavy, and the personal with the political, to keep people engaged and open to dialogue.

Lavin shared his personal story and his concerns about the direction of the national discourse on guns:

Having been born in Ecuador, a country where democracy historically has seemed optional, I've always held the experiment that is our US democracy in the highest regard. It's why I'm so excited to listen to this conversation. This is special. In my twenty-five years as a journalist, I haven't seen anything like this before. Honored to be among the moderators here.

I started off in L.A. as a music and culture writer, then moved to [New] Jersey, where most of my career has been at the state's biggest paper and news website. There I've worn many hats, including editor of the arts/features section, reader engagement director and now an opinion editor. Why did I move from sunny southern Cal to snow-in-April New Jersey? Love. My wife, who is from Poland, and I have been married for nearly twenty years. We have an amazing 11-year-old girl and 10-year-old boy. We make art and go fishing together. I also coach my son's soccer team, and I'm a Cub Scout den leader. Like most parents, we want a brighter future for them.

After meeting and hearing from the folks who joined us in Washington, DC, for this project, I'm feeling optimistic about that future. I believe we're all going to learn new things here.

Despite the hope that conversation would go smoothly on its own, he and the other moderators labored behind the scenes to do what they could to make sure that the conversation was as fruitful as possible for everyone involved.

The other moderators and support team had also been preparing for their roles, which, in many ways, involved preparing for the unknown. While they would be building on the model that Spaceship Media created and had implemented many times before, the topic of guns hadn't been addressed before. And for most of the participants, moderators, and reporters, the Spaceship Media method was also new.

Parisa Parsa from Essential Partners worked with the moderators on how to have sensitive conversations with participants. A project like the "Guns" conversation simply can't happen, she noted, "without thoughtful facilitation."

Lavin, who had met the participants in Washington, DC, noted "magical moments" where people connected over gaping divides. He was excited to help nurture more connections. He was equally enthused, as were other moderators, to be offered an "opportunity for deep listening and the chance to hone a new skill for journalists, helping facilitate civil conversation in a new way."

Moderator Brittney Walker Pettigrew had been a participant in the Talking Politics Project in 2016 and knew there would be some storms before people would be able to hear one another.

She had seen discussions like this before. The beginnings can be chaotic, she said, especially when helping group members try a new way of communicating. "What emerges on the other side is a clean machine," she said.

For "Guns, An American Conversation," Walker Pettigrew was recruited as a moderator both because of the skills she had developed through her career as a social worker, and her experience as a participant.

In discussing what was happening behind the scenes of the Facebook conversation, she said, "Our moderator chat was on fire all day. . . . We would screenshot a post and say 'what do people want to do' . . . and the chat for options would begin."

As posts started rolling in she didn't know she herself would soon have a challenging, life-changing experience.

The first thing Brittany and the other moderators did was try to bring together more than one hundred new participants with the group that had met in person in DC. One new participant, antigun activist Helene Bludman, introduced herself to the group with a clear message:

> I am turning 65 later this month. Married, three children, one grandchild. Born and raised in south-eastern Pennsylvania where I still reside.
>
> I'm going to be honest. I have a deep seated fear and mistrust of guns, especially the AR-15, because they are powerful weapons that can cause large scale death or maiming to innocent people. The escalating level of gun violence in our country has only exacerbated that fear. I am a liberal and support progressive causes.
>
> That said, I recognize that polarization on the gun issue is not helping me nor our country. I am going to be open minded and read thoughtfully what others have to say. I sincerely hope that the

worst case scenario will be that we agree to disagree, and perhaps even move a bit more to the center than before.

I hope what I have said has not offended anyone. If it has, I apologize.

Adrian Moy, another of those who had gathered in DC, checked in from Oregon. A grandfather and train operator looking forward to retirement, Moy described himself as a "casual (gun) owner and sometime (wanna do it more) small bore target shooter; also have pistols and shotguns; believe in 2nd amendment and self-defense."

He noted that most of the people in his circle of friends and relatives are avid gun enthusiasts and react negatively to any discussion involving "gun control." But he saw the possibility of some middle ground. "I believe some regulations are just plain common sense," he said, "and I am hopeful this discussion will lead to a discovery of what is acceptable and practical vis-a-vis lawmaking and enforcement. Wish us luck."

Luck was needed in some cases, as the discussion was constantly evolving, often moving so quickly—and at all hours—that it could be challenging for participants to keep up with the latest, most interesting, most enlightening, or most amusing conversations of the previous twenty-four hours. As Michelle Holmes described it, it was "like a house with a big party going on, and lots of conversation in different rooms." The Advance team created a daily, conversational-style newsletter, authored by Stephen Koff with input from moderators, to deal with the challenge. Several times over the course of a month, people who were especially vocal or aggressive were asked to be silent for a while to let others have a say. A handful of times, participants were asked to leave the group altogether. Moderators walked a careful tightrope, working in real time as cheerleaders, ringleaders, and disciplinarians, often simultaneously.

Part of that balancing act was helping to facilitate productive conversations between participants with differing opinions. It often went better than many had anticipated.

• • •

As he did in DC, and would do throughout the conversation, Louisiana lawyer and Second Amendment stalwart Dan Zelenka jumped in with one of the first posts to generate a significant response.

The post was a primer on America's array of guns and why such weapons as the AR-15 should be made available:

> Why does the public need access to any rifle? Rifles are used for hunting big and small game and predators. They are used for target shooting and personal defense. And they are used for plinking (shooting for fun).
>
> Now imagine a rifle that was designed with a modular platform that could do all of those things not just in an OK manner but really well. Also imagine that it could be adjusted to fit everybody [*sic*] style and did not recoil at a level that would bother even a novice shooter.

The rifle I just described is the AR-15. It is the most popular rifle in the US because it can be configured to do all of those things well.

I have for years engaged in rifle competition at a national level. . . . As a hunting rifle, they can be chambered in a number of different calibers appropriate for deer or coyotes or hogs or even squirrels. The stock can even be adjusted to fit both short and tall people.

As a defensive rifle, the AR-15 excels. For home defense, it is far better than a pistol because it is easier to hit with and the bullets penetrate less than a pistol. Both of these are important because you want the bad guy to be hit and stopped but no one else. You are responsible for every bullet you shoot. . . .

They are fun to shoot.

Semi automatic firearms have been available to the public since the 1880s. The self loading mechanism is used in rifles, pistols and shotguns. The AR-15 specifically has been sold to the public since 1963. I bought my first one in 1978. When Colt's patent ran out in the early 1990s, many different manufacturers began building AR-15 type rifles. Currently, nearly every firearm manufacturer in the US makes this type of rifle. It is the most popular rifle with 8–10 million in private hands. The US Supreme Court test to determine whether a particular type of firearm is protected by the 2nd amendment is whether it is in common use by civilians. Clearly semi automatics in general and the AR-15 in particular meet that test.

So we have a protected firearm that is extremely useful for a number of legal purposes. The question isn't why does the public need an AR-15, but why wouldn't they?

As a law-abiding American we not only have the right to keep and bear arms but we have the right to choose the one that we believe suits us best. To put it another way, you don't need a Porsche to go to the grocery; but you certainly have the right to drive one if you want.

A key piece of Spaceship Media's dialogue journalism is to supply reporting for the conversations in direct response to the questions and issues that arise in the group in pieces known as FactStacks. As such, the guns team was ready to answer requests to provide information about topics the participants wished to explore. Melanie Jeffcoat, who had survived a school shooting when she was younger, and was an active member of Moms Demand Action, a grassroots group advocating for safety measures to help end gun violence, asked the staff for some illumination on the type of guns Zelenka was referencing.

Here is what the reporters produced:

Assault Weapons and Automatic Firearms: Some Definitions

What an Assault Weapon Is and Isn't

"Assault weapon" is a term used somewhat loosely in the public conversation about firearms. The gun industry's traditional definition of an "assault rifle" is a weapon the military generally uses and has "select fire capabilities," or the "capability to switch between semi-automatic or a fully automatic mode," CNBC reported in February 2018.[4]

When the federal government had an assault weapon ban from 1994 to 2004, it had a lengthy glossary of what was included, including fully automatic weapons.[5]

But it also included semiautomatic rifles that had an ability to accept a detachable magazine—if the rifle had at least two of certain features, such as a folding or telescoping stock, or a pistol grip that protruded conspicuously beneath the action of the weapon. (The law, which has since expired, had numerous exceptions. We will provide a separate look at that federal ban and studies on how it worked.)

Seven states and the District of Columbia have their own laws on assault weapons, according to the Giffords Law Center to Prevent Gun Violence. One of them is California, which defines an assault rifle as a semiautomatic, center-fire rifle that does not have a fixed magazine but has any one of the following[6]:

- A pistol grip that protrudes conspicuously beneath the action of the weapon.
- A thumbhole stock.
- A folding or telescoping stock.
- A grenade launcher or flare launcher.
- A flash suppressor.
- A forward pistol grip.

California also includes under its assault weapons definitions a semiautomatic, center-fire rifle that has a fixed magazine with the capacity to accept more than ten rounds, and a semiautomatic, center-fire rifle that has an overall length of less than thirty inches.

What an Automatic Firearm Does

Fully automatic weapons fire repeated rounds with the single pull of a trigger. These are also referred to as machine guns, and machine guns are illegal, expensive, and hard to get in most civilian applications.

"An assault rifle is fully automatic—a machine gun. Automatic firearms have been severely restricted from civilian ownership since 1934," says the National Shooting Sports Federation, a firearms industry trade group.[7]

What a Semiautomatic Firearm Does

A semiautomatic fires once with each pull of the trigger, according to gun-rights and sports-shooting groups including the Buckeye Firearms Association in Ohio. Some automatic and semiautomatic weapons look alike, but they operate differently.[8]

A semiautomatic firearm automatically reloads the chamber with a cartridge from a magazine after each shot and is ready to fire again, says Politifact and a number of sport shooting groups. This allows for rounds to be fired as rapidly as someone can pull the trigger if ammunition is in the magazine.[9]

How Rapidly a Semiautomatic Weapon Can Realistically Fire

Tom Kehoe, a Florida firearms instructor and leather holster maker, wrote in a Quora post that top sporting competitors can pull the trigger "three times a second—for short periods of time. So the theoretical 'cycling rate' might be 180 rounds per minute, but the reality is you're only maintaining it for bursts of a second or two."[10]

Rapid firing generates tremendous amounts of heat, he wrote, and most modern semi-automatic weapons use thirty-round magazines, "which means the mag would have to be changed six times to reach the magic 180 number. An expert can change a mag on some rifles in about two to three seconds (depending on the gun and how he/she has staged the mags), but that's still 12–18 seconds of lost shooting time per minute."

That would make the maximum theoretical rate about 138 rounds per minute, he said.

How a Bump Stock Can Alter That

A bump stock is a device that attaches to a semi-automatic weapon and uses its recoil to fire more rapidly, explains *Popular Mechanics*. "So long as a shooter maintains forward pressure, the rifle will continue to fire at a rate much faster than could be accomplished with even the quickest possible series of manual trigger pulls."[11]

Phrased slightly differently, a "bump stock" replaces a rifle's standard stock, which is the part held against the shoulder. It frees the weapon to slide back and forth rapidly, harnessing the energy from the kickback shooters feel when the weapon fires. This is from a *New York Times* explanation of how they work.[12]

Bump stocks became better known to the public after they were found in Stephen Paddock's Las Vegas hotel room following the October 1, 2017, shooting of outdoor concert goers. Fifty-eight people were killed and hundreds were reported wounded.

Bump stocks are legal, with the US Bureau of Alcohol, Tobacco, Firearms, and Explosives giving an opinion in 2010 that since they were gun parts but not actual weapons, bump stocks could not be regulated under existing laws prohibiting certain firearms.

A number of groups, including the National Rifle Association, say that needs to change. "The NRA believes that devices designed to allow semi-automatic rifles to function like fully-automatic rifles should be subject to additional regulations," the NRA said in a statement.[13]

President Donald Trump said in February 2018 that he wanted the Justice Department to look into regulating bump stocks, and on March 10, 2018, Attorney General Jeff Sessions issued a notice of a proposed regulation "to clarify that the definition of machine gun in the National Firearms Act and Gun Control Act includes bump stock type devices, and that federal law accordingly prohibits the possession, sale, or manufacture of such devices."[14]

Where the AR-15 Fits In

The civilian AR-15, which has appeared in mass shootings including the one that killed seventeen people at a Parkland, Florida, high school in February 2018, has only semiautomatic settings. A bump stock was not used in those shootings. The "AR" part of the firearm's name does not mean assault rifle. Rather, it stands for ArmaLite rifle, after the company that developed it in the 1950s.

The AR-15 is popular among hobbyists, with one in five firearms purchased in this country an AR-style weapon, according to National Shooting Sports Foundation figures cited by NBC News. It is sleek, delivering a gratifying blast of adrenaline, and a symbol, the embodiment of core American values—freedom, might, self-reliance, NBC said after interviewing a number of gun owners.[15]

Gun control advocates say the AR-15 has

a high muzzle velocity, which, combined with the small .223 round, "produces a violent ricochet through an animal body if it hits bone," the *Washington Post* reported.[16]

But the AR-15 can be adopted for different uses and kinds of hunting. The National Shooting Sports Foundation says that because the AR-15 platform is modular, able to affix different "uppers" (barrel and chamber), its ammunition capability can include ".22, .223 (5.56 x 45mm), 6.8 SPC, .308, .450 Bushmaster and about a dozen others. Upper receivers for pistol calibers such as 9 mm, .40, and .45 are available. There are even .410 shotgun versions," the foundation says.

AR-15-style rifles "are no more powerful than other hunting rifles of the same caliber," the foundation says.[17]

Several group members balked at Zelenka saying how much fun it is to shoot an AR-15.

One participant responded to Zelenka's post: "What if I found it fun to shoot a shoulder-fired missile? Should all 'arms' be protected under the 2A? I think we can all agree that some regulation of 'arms' is good."

Melanie Jeffcoat, who had asked for additional reporting earlier, jumped in as well:

I have heard they are fun to shoot and I appreciate you outlining the other uses. I have always wondered why they couldn't be limited to shooting ranges so that people can enjoy the sensation of shooting the weapon in a secured environment but perhaps they aren't as widely available. Although there may be millions out there, we have no idea how many of them are in the hands of reasonable people like yourself. I am not a hunter so I can't speak to how it helps in that area but I do wonder why a weapon like that is needed to kill a deer or a squirrel. Wouldn't it be harder (and more challenging) to use a traditional rifle? And I am genuinely asking. I have never hunted.

Zelenka replied:

Melanie, all good questions. I am going to start with the hunting one. Let me first say that any hunter worth the title attempts to kill his/her prey with a single shot. I and many of my friends have used the AR-15-style rifle for hunting for years and I don't recall personally using more than one shot. If a follow-up shot is needed or there are multiple targets like a founder of hogs being able to take a second or third accurate shot without having to disturb your sight picture is a significant plus.

As a hunting rifle, the AR-15 has a few other attributes. It is light, accurate, doesn't recoil much and can be adjusted to fit the shooter's body or even make up the difference between light clothing and heavy clothing.

In the circular nature of Facebook posts, threads branched onto other topics and came back around. Jeffcoat and Zelenka went back and forth several times, culminating with Jeffcoat again asking the staff to do some research to illuminate some areas of disagreement.

Adrian Moy said the AR-15 rifles are so popular that banning them wouldn't make a difference. Banning them would "only do one thing," he contended—cause a spike in sales because of the "they're coming to take my guns away" fearmongering. "The AR-15 gets a bad rap but the semiautomatic versions function just like any other semiautomatic rifle. There are other rifles out there much more powerful (bigger loads, bigger bullets, longer range, etc.) than the AR-15. Most of my friends and relatives already have an AR-15, and until recently I was hot to have one myself."

In total, Zelenka's post prompted fifty comments, and he had a rapid-fire response to nearly every question asked of him.

But despite his firm stance as a Second Amendment defender, Zelenka was far from the only gun-rights advocate ready to step in and address the other side. Sometimes, as happens with tough topics, sensitivities were broached and lines were crossed without the commenter seemingly knowing why others might find their comment or observation offensive.

In a particularly notable conversation, for example, a gun-rights advocate posted that those on his side had a deep need to protect the Second Amendment, just like civil rights icon Rosa Parks needed to sit at the front of the bus.

When Brittany Walker Pettigrew saw the post, she said, "I wanted to quit at that moment."

She followed the advice the moderators had repeated several times to the group: If you find yourself feeling defensive, step back and take a different approach. Instead of telling others why they're wrong (or why you're right), explore why they have a perspective that's different from yours.

Walker Pettigrew eventually had a late-night, one-on-one chat with the Second Amendment defender to explain why the remark was offensive. After the initial shock had worn off, she saw a sliver of what the commenter was hoping to get across. What started as a conversation about guns brought the California social worker and the gun-rights defender to unexpected common ground, as they bonded over the shared history of feeling treated like second-class citizens.

Ultimately she said she saw that the tough-talking gun advocate felt like much of the country is often openly hostile to Second Amendment defenders. He told her how hard it was for those defenders to hear "crowds of people at an anti-gun protest saying 'fuck the NRA.'"

She told him that by invoking a revered figure such as Parks, he was distracting from his main point.

It was a poignant moment; what could have blown up with acrimony turned instead to understanding. Walker Pettigrew was glad she'd kept her composure, as she felt like she'd been true to the spirit of the broader tone of the conversation. As she told the gun-rights supporter, "Discomfort is where growth occurs. We can't start healing until we find the injury." She didn't know until later that what she'd done would soon feel more momentous than that.

After that late-night conversation, Walker Pettigrew had a dream.

She was sitting on some porch steps when a visitor came. It was an older African American woman. They shared iced tea in what felt like a calm, accepting bubble.

When she woke up, she said, "I felt like I'd been visited."

At first she couldn't quite place the familiar face in the dream. Then, she said, "it occurred to me that the face was in a picture in my house. It was my great-grandmother, Rosie."

Rosie had been a slave. A set of iced tea glasses was one of the few worldly goods she had passed along over the generations.

And Walker Pettigrew now had them. In the dream, they drank from those glasses on the porch steps.

"It was like she was saying, 'You are doing something I could never do,'" she said. "It's like she was saying to me 'You are doing something *none* of us could ever do.'"

For the first time, the lifelong social worker who every day championed what's best for others had stood up directly for herself, her family, and her ancestors, such as Rosie.

She'd never before been in a space safe enough to take such action. "That dream was really powerful for me," she said.

Walker Pettigrew called her dad to share her experience. He agreed that she had done something extraordinary.

What started as a conversation about guns ended up being the moment that gave her the courage to make herself heard.

Chapter 3

Bringing to mind issues of life and death, community rights, class and race divides, personal tragedies, and fears about the future, very often the conversation surrounding guns and gun rights stirs up intense emotions. That intensity tends to overshadow some of the less emotionally loaded aspects of the larger guns conversation. While not as emotionally propelling, the everyday, routine aspects of gun ownership are essential aspects of understanding the viewpoints of gun owners.

A few weeks into the exercise, the Facebook group took a brief foray into one such frequently overlooked facet of the gun conversation: how to dress for concealment and carry success. Many members of the group who carry a concealed weapon regularly take their guns with them nearly everywhere. It impacts not only what they wear, but in some ways, how they act in public. It becomes a representation of how they present themselves to the world.

Bruce Packard, a progressive member of the group whose attitude toward guns had evolved during his life, kicked off the conversation: "Sometimes, you may choose the correct outfit, but may lean or bend over and your gun's outline may show ('print'). If a criminal sees this, they may take your weapon and now it is a threat to you and the public. Thoughts?"

Zekiye Mary Salman, from Lansing, Michigan, came to the gun conversation with an educational background in gender and ethics and with work experience helping communities find solutions to fight poverty. In the concealed-carry wardrobe conversation, she offered that "my partner's sister is a state trooper and carries constantly and she had to buy a whole new wardrobe to conceal her weapon (especially high-waisted pants).

"She also always wears looser tops and layers so that even if her weapon does show she has another layer to conceal it. This makes me think about different ways of existing in the world and how that changes just by having a gun. She, for instance, ALWAYS sits in the seat that faces the door when we go out to restaurants."

In her self-introduction to the group, Salman also mentioned that she was interested in learning more about progun advocates, so she added a few questions to this later post: "How does carrying impact daily decisions that we might not think about? How does it impact how you walk in the world? How does it impact how you occupy space? Do you ever mourn the loss of some of the freedom that comes with NOT carrying a gun (for example, I imagine, especially with training, you don't stop seeing what are the best positions to shoot from if it were necessary)?"

Dan Zelenka weighed in: "Carrying every day is a pain in the butt. You clearly must dress around it. I buy my pants [one inch] larger in the waist to accommodate my holster. I even have my tailor fit my suit and sports coats with my gun on so they drape correctly. I also have multiple holster types and even several different guns to handle all dress situations. It may be hard to hide a full-sized Glock during a New Orleans summer, but you can stuff a small automatic in a pocket holster in almost any loose-fitting pair of pants or shorts with biggish pockets. I would rather buy a new wardrobe than go anywhere unarmed, but that is just me."

Don Alley, a self-defense, personal protection, and shooting instructor who describes himself as "pro-freedom and pro-'nonaggression,'" said "freedom means just how we do that is left to the individual, and individuals attempting to dictate how others will satisfy these means of doing so are overstepping their authority." He used his background to offer some insights:

1. Concealed definitely means concealed. Clothing that is a bit baggy is preferred. Dark clothing or light clothing with patterns disrupts the eye and helps concealability. Either way, your firearm, method of carry, holster, and clothing work as a *** system *** to ensure concealed means concealed.

2. Printing is a minor concern, really. It's amazing how little people pay attention anyways. We live in an era where a lady walked into a fountain because she was on her phone. =) That being said, it is still your responsibility to do due diligence to stay concealed. In MI, open carry is legal so printing or exposure is not a crime. Other states may vary.

3. Bad guy sees: The odds of printing and being noticed is small. The odds of being noticed AND it's a criminal are very small. The odds of a criminal deciding to go after you are extremely small. He is looking for an easy target, not you specifically. In general, he'll let you go on your way and find an easy mark. That being said, firearms should be only 1 facet of your personal protection strategy. Pick up some martial training as well. My company teaches the firearm is last-resort only, and do a number of classes to ensure our students have skills for when the firearm is not justifiable.

Although not as impassioned or heated as some of the other threads in the group, the discussion surrounding clothing and its restrictions nevertheless represented a serious split. As they had noted, many of the participants with a conceal-carry permit rarely left their home without a weapon. Those participants who actively carried most often cited the Second

Amendment as supporting their right to bear concealed arms, in states where it is allowed.

The other side wondered if they didn't have a right to expect to be in a gun-free space.

Perhaps spurred on by the divides that the concealed-carry conversation highlighted, the discussion quickly got serious.

As the gun conversation evolved within the Facebook group, the core dynamics essentially remained steady. At one end were the gun-rights advocates who believe that all talk about restricting gun access has one ultimate dismissal point: the Second Amendment.

On the other end of the spectrum were antigun activists who not only questioned how any type of weapon should be out in the world unless used for law enforcement, but challenged whether they should be out in the world in the first place.

Over time, the gap between those extremes was increasingly filled by participants who voiced more nuanced positions and who were increasingly willing to engage with others.

At the same time, alliances were starting to form. People who were already inclined to push back against ideas pushed back even harder. The mostly behind-the-curtains cajoling of participants by moderators and staff also occasionally became more pointed.

As part of a strategy laid out in Spaceship Media's methods to help prompt productive conversation, moderators were clicking that "like" button a bit more often, working to keep members of the group inspired and keep the conversation productive. It was a nonstop process.

Responding to the divides that emerged as a result of the concealed-carry conversation and hoping to clarify some key terms, facts, and figures, Stephen Koff directly addressed the laws surrounding concealed-carry laws in a piece created for Advance Local's sites:

Gun owners are frustrated by conflicting concealed-carry laws: *Guns, An American Conversation*[1]

WASHINGTON: Mark Squid is licensed in Virginia to carry a concealed gun. Dan Zelenka has a similar license from Louisiana.

Both men are law-abiding. Both enjoy firearms sports and support the right to carry a weapon safely for hunting, target practice, or personal and family protection. By carrying a gun out of public view, they present no apparent threat to others, gun-rights activists say.

But whether they truly have a good reason to carry a concealed weapon is a matter of debate in some states—and some states are pickier about this than others.

That means gun owners with concealed-weapons permits from states such as Virginia, Louisiana, Alabama, Michigan, and Ohio must leave their firearms at home when traveling to places such as New York, California, New Jersey, and Maryland.

In those states, so-called concealed-carry permits are issued relatively sparingly—sometimes only if someone can prove a justifiable need such as a threat to his or her safety—and permits from other states aren't recognized. Otherwise, these out-of-staters risk being charged criminally if stopped by police and searched.

A similar problem occurs when Squid or Zelenka wants to go to the nation's capital, because even though a federal appeals court in 2017 struck down the District of Columbia's "good reason" requirement for obtaining a permit, the city still won't recognize permits issued elsewhere.

The legal ability to carry a concealed weapon into another state is governed by a web of complex state laws and interstate reciprocity agreements. An Ohioan with a concealed-carry license can go into Michigan, Pennsylvania, Indiana, Kentucky, and West Virginia without any problems, for example, according to the Ohio attorney general's office. But if this gun owner was caught carrying his concealed weapon in Illinois, he'd face trouble.[2]

This is why Zelenka, an attorney, and Squid,

a nickname used by a navy veteran participating in a nationwide dialogue on guns, support the Concealed Carry Reciprocity Act of 2017.

The bill, which the Republican-led House of Representatives passed almost entirely along party lines in December, would declare that every state must recognize the right to concealed carry if the gun holder got a license in another state.

This issue has come up twice—by proponents and opponents—in "Guns, An American Conversation," an initiative by Advance Local newsrooms from across the country in partnership with Spaceship Media. The project has brought together 150 engaged readers with a broad spectrum of opinions to talk about guns in an honest and civil way through a closed Facebook group.

All participants quoted in this story agreed to have their comments appear on the record, but Squid asked that his nickname be used rather than his real name because he discussed traveling from his home state to see family members, some with sensitive government-related job security clearances.

Today's Topic:
Concealed-Carry Reciprocity

Each state sets its own standards for concealed-carry permits, and local authorities in some jurisdictions get a say in approval or denial. That's how some officials, and police chiefs, say it should be.

The International Association of Chiefs of Police, which represents eighteen thousand police departments in the United States, sent a letter on the topic to Congress on April 19, 2018.

The letter said that to allow people to freely cross state boundaries with their weapons, even if licensed in a different state, would be "a dangerous encroachment on individual state efforts to protect public safety, and it would effectively nullify duly enacted state laws and hamper law enforcement efforts to prevent gun violence.

"Mandated reciprocity would effectively override the permitting requirements of individual states, such as requiring safety training or prohibiting permits for people with multiple convictions for violent misdemeanors or drug or alcohol abuse problems," the letter said.

Melanie Jeffcoat of Homewood, Alabama, a member of the "Guns, An American Conversation" group, described a local situation she said exemplified the potential problem with nation-wide concealed-carry reciprocity, or CCR. "An abused woman left this state because she feared for her life from her gun-owning ex-boyfriend," she said. "And she didn't report the abuse (not uncommon), but simply left him.

"She moves to NY or CT or a state with the strictest laws possible. What if CCR is passed? She again lives in fear that he would be within his rights to travel to her new state with his gun.

"Yes, he could do it illegally but this would allow the rights to be on his side. Not hers."

Yet a welcoming view toward reciprocity was voiced by twenty-four state attorneys general, including those of Ohio, Michigan, Alabama, and Louisiana. In a letter to congressional leaders in December 2017, they lamented that ten states refuse to recognize out-of-state concealed carry permits, "and many more refuse to recognize out-of-state concealed carry permits unless certain conditions are met."

"The citizen interest in self-defense, supported and protected by the Second Amendment, is called into serious question by such blanket refusals to permit carrying firearms in self-defense outside the home or to allow non-resident visitors to carry concealed weapons," the attorneys general said. Concealed-carry reciprocity is so important to gun-rights activists that the National Rifle Association calls it its "highest legislative priority" in Congress. But passage could be difficult in the Senate, where Republican sponsors have a smaller majority than in the House. Even if the bill passed, individual states would still have the right to limit where someone with a permit could carry his or her weapon. "You'd have to abide by all the laws of the state that you are in," an NRA spokeswoman said.[3]

[The House bill that passed in 2017 never advanced to the Senate floor. Republicans in both houses of Congress reintroduced concealed-carry reciprocity bills in January 2019, but they faced even longer odds with the House now in Democratic hands and members wanting more gun control, not less.]

Inside the Conversation

Members of the "Guns, An American Conversation" group took up the issue on two different occasions: once when raised by Jeffcoat, and once when David Preston, of Mobile, Alabama, presented a copy of the reciprocity bill and asked members what they thought. Here's some of the online dialogue that followed.[4]

Zekiye Mary Salman, of Lansing, Michigan: "Aside from 'it's my right,' which I understand as an argument, why might people be taking guns from one state to another? Just taking it on family vacation? It's an unrelated question but as a non-gun owner I'd be interested in hearing some perspectives on why putting time and energy into this issue in terms of legislation is important and a priority."

Mark Squid, of Virginia Beach, Virginia: "I would carry across state lines for the same reason I carry at home, it's a tool in my tool kit of preparedness."

Salman: "Have you had negative experiences with carrying in other states or do you currently just leave everything at home to avoid laws? If so, are there specific instances when you'd be traveling that you would sit down and get up to date on everything (or double-check) and make that burdensome work worthwhile?"

Squid: "An example of a burden, I live in Virginia Beach, Va. and travel to Frederick, MD, where I have relatives, almost every holiday and a couple times in the summer. My sister also lives in Baltimore, MD, and we meet up in DC quite often for lunch. Maryland does not recognize any other state's permits, nor does DC.

"For the trip to Maryland I can disarm and store the firearm as long as it is done before entering MD. For DC trips, I must leave behind as there is no provision in any law for me as non-resident of DC to even have possession of a firearm, let alone carry one."

Todd Bozes, of Fountain Hill, Pennsylvania: "I had a friend who posted PA's concealed carry info that included all of the state's reciprocity agreements. It is a 49 page document with a bunch of different lists of which states it is legal to carry a concealed weapon under different circumstances. My major take away from it was questioning how it is reasonably expected for people to keep track of all these laws, especially since many could be changing. It seems overly complicated considering the severity of the penalties for carrying illegally. Based on that, I think that I've at least become more supportive of steps being taken to simplify things, whatever that may look like."

Joe Vargo, of Columbus, Ohio: "100% against. That makes the whole country have to live with the consequences of the least regulated state. And I think a major case can be made for the harms of carrying guns to a society."

Ellen Boegel, of Long Island, New York: "This question gets to the heart of states' rights and the exact nature of the Second Amendment, which makes it difficult to answer. States traditionally have the authority to enact public health and safety laws and the Supreme Court decisions upholding a personal Second Amendment right acknowledge states may use this authority to restrict gun ownership and usage.

"I personally would support national reciprocity only when all states enact strict carry requirements. Those requirements would include background checks for criminal convictions and mental health dangerousness evaluations, mandatory gun safety courses, ammunition limitations, and regular re-evaluation (similar to eye tests for driver's licenses)."

John Noel Bartlett, of Oil City, Pennsylvania: "I'm not in favor of simple reciprocity. It's my belief that setting standards and requirements for concealed carry does not violate the 2nd Amendment and is within the scope of restrictions likely to be permitted by the courts. So, if one state allows concealed carry with only minimum requirements and another has much stricter, I think that should be allowed.

"Now, it might be possible for every state to offer a reciprocal license in addition to its in-state license by meeting the standards of the strictest state. Convoluted I know and probably not practical. I'm quite uncomfortable with how easy it is to get a CCP in my state, and I have one. I think you should need to show some basic proficiency and knowledge of what is appropriate and inappropriate."

Dan Zelenka, of Covington, Louisiana: "Louisiana has reciprocity with 38 or 39 other states. I don't travel to states that do not recognize Louisiana's CHP [concealed handgun permit] without some sort of coercion, i.e., my job depends on it or agreeing to go to DC for this gun group. There is nothing that I left in New Jersey or New York that I need to go there for.

The only hardship I have is Napa being in California which is a no-travel zone. Sometimes my wife coerces me."

Rev. Kris Eggert, of South Euclid, Ohio: "I am personally opposed and our organization, God Before Guns, is also opposed. We have called and written our Reps and Senators, and we advocated against in the Halls of Congress. It removes state control and it creates the worst common denominator as states with the most lax requirements would rule."

Peter Lotto, of Fayetteville, New York: "There is no reason why people in one state should tolerate guns being carried by tourists or travelers who would be denied a permit in that state."

Vargo: "What are some cases in which a person from out of state would need to bring a gun with them on a trip? I can't imagine people are taking vacations to places they would fear for their safety, and at least here, most businesses prohibit weapons of any kind, so you couldn't bring a gun if you're traveling for business."

Zelenka: "All places, in all circumstances. Just because I carry a gun doesn't mean I fear for my safety. I carry one when I travel because one never knows what may happen. I carry one when I hike because one may run into 2 legged or 4 legged predators. I carry one when I travel for business. I work for myself so I make the rules. I would rather have it and not need it than need it and not have it. It is like a spare tire, fire extinguisher, tourniquet, first aid kit."

Vargo: "Do you avoid visiting places where it's not legal to carry?"

Zelenka: "Yes!"

Eggert: "Then our paths will probably never cross!"

Zelenka: "Never can tell. I go to Port Clinton, Ohio most years."

Eggert: "It would be fine to meet each other. Just a joke since I will choose a place that doesn't allow guns to ones that do."

Zelenka: "A bar. I never drink and carry."

In the published piece Zelenka had the last word. But it was not the last word on the topic. One of the core beliefs that guides Spaceship Media's work is the idea that, when given structure and support in doing so, people can talk about the difficult issues that divide them. If that's the case, the conceal-carry conversation was certainly part of the next step. The next one got a little sharper, and truths were held a little tighter. But some participants could see changes within themselves.

Helene Cohen Bludman is a sixty-five-year-old grand-mother from southeastern Pennsylvania who introduced herself to the group like this: "I have a deep seated fear and mistrust of guns, especially the AR-15, because they are powerful weapons that can cause large scale death or maiming to innocent people." But this far into the conversation, she surprised even herself with her shifting attitudes.

"I had somewhat of an epiphany last night," she posted. "I am on a committee that is organizing a Gun Violence Awareness Day in my community. The committee members are nice, normal people. As we went through the agenda, they passed out a sheet of paper with some suggested content for protest signs. And I cringed. Now, I wouldn't have batted an eye before at these. Like, 'The NRA is Evil.' But now things are different. Did I say anything? No. I had to process it first. But I recognized a shift in my thinking that took me by surprise. I thank you all for contributing to this new awareness. Can anyone else relate to this?"

Many of the quieter participants weighed on Bludman's question, echoing their own shift in views. Progun advocate

Eric Traux noted, "I can relate for sure. My stance on waiting periods alone is a moving target in my mind. I am much quicker to listen now."

Reba Holley, a gun control advocate from New Jersey, noted, "I'd say I haven't changed my opinion about guns or what I think needs to be done, but I measure my words differently when talking about it."

Clearly the active discussions were having an impact on the participants effectively listening and engaging.

Kris Eggert reminded the group that gun violence was claiming lives even as the group was making some progress within their Facebook discussion. She referenced a sobering article about a seventeen-year-old who was killed.

> If we posted every death from guns from yesterday, there could be more than 100 more (according to the latest stats from the CDC—106 die every day).
>
> Just a reminder that while we take this 4-week period to discuss the issue and try to find common ground, thousands will die and probably twice that number will be injured. It's my hope and my daily prayer that discussions such as these move us to action before more thousands needlessly die.[5]

Based on the discussions surrounding gun violence, Stephen Koff created a FactStack breaking down gun deaths by the numbers. It was a stark look at the tragedy that gun violence can create.

How Gun Deaths Are Counted

The Number of Firearms Deaths in the United States[6]

The US Centers for Disease Control and Prevention, or CDC, tracks deaths in the United States by cause. The latest full year's worth of data covers 2016. In raw numbers, here are total firearms deaths in the United States over five years, via data from the CDC.

2012: 33,563
2013: 33,636
2014: 33,594
2015: 36,252
2016: 38,658

How That Changes When Accounting for Our Growing Population

The CDC puts the numbers in context by calculating them on the basis of population (deaths per 100,000 people). It also adjusts that rate based on the age of the United States population, which some authorities say is a more meaningful figure when looking at deaths from all causes because incidences of some deaths differ by age. The differences in the per-capita rates involving gun deaths are relatively slight.

2012: 10.69 firearm deaths per 100,000 people, or 10.45 on an age-adjusted basis
2013: 10.64 firearm deaths per 100,000 people, or 10.38 on an age-adjusted basis
2014: 10.55 firearm deaths per 100,000 people, or 10.26 on an age-adjusted basis
2015: 11.30 firearm deaths per 100,000 people, or 11.03 on an age-adjusted basis
2016: 11.96 gun deaths per 100,000 people, or 11.73 on an age-adjusted basis

The Breakdown for Homicide, Suicide, and Other Gun Deaths

In 2016, firearms deaths were counted this way by the CDC:

- **Suicide:** 59.3 percent of gun deaths, or 22,938 in raw numbers.
- **Homicide:** 37.28 percent of gun deaths, or 14,415 in raw numbers.*
- **Legal Intervention:** 1.31 percent of gun deaths, or 510 in raw numbers, were legal interventions, which means deaths as a

result of police interaction. These include deaths by gunfire as well as what is loosely known as "suicide by cop," in which someone intentionally provokes law enforcement to the point of gunfire.*[7]

- **Unintentional Shootings:** 1.28 percent of gun deaths, or 495 in raw numbers, were classified as unintentional.
- **Undetermined:** 0.77 percent of gun deaths, or 300 in raw numbers, resulted from undetermined intent.

* Data for homicides and legal interventions are counted together in some analyses, and the CDC makes such a method of counting available. We have chosen to give a fuller breakdown, as provided by the CDC.

How the Homicide Rate Changed in Recent Years

Academic studies and media reports described a spike in big-city homicides in 2015 and 2016. CDC data bear this out.[8]

In 2015, 35.8 percent of gun deaths were attributed to homicides. In 2016, 37.28 percent were.

But in 2014, a lower share of gun deaths—32.76 percent—were from homicides, and 33.3 percent were in 2013. The share was slightly higher one year earlier—in 2012—when 34.62 percent of gun deaths in the United States were categorized as homicides, but that still was lower than in 2016. To make an apples-to-apples comparison, there were 11,622 homicide deaths involving firearms in 2012, for an age-adjusted rate of 3.76 firearm-homicides per 100,000 population. But by 2016, the number of homicides with firearms reached 14,415, for an age-adjusted rate of 4.60 per 100,000 population. As a raw number, that's not large. As a change in the rate, it is.

But that's just five years of data.

Longer-Term Trends

CDC databases allow for comparisons dating to 1981. A comparison of the 35-year span of data, 1981 to 2016, show deaths from guns have dropped dramatically, and so have the share attributable to homicides. The numbers here are for firearms deaths per 100,000 population, age-adjusted, and corresponding rates strictly for firearms homicides.

Year	Total Firearms Death Rate	Firearms Homicide Rate
1981	14.64	6.34
1991	14.82	6.64
2001	10.31	3.93
2011	10.16	3.59
2016	11.73	4.60

Notice the dramatic drop in homicides by 2001? What happened?

The Pew Research Center said in a report that demographics played a role. "The outsized post–World War II baby boom, which produced a large number of people in the high-crime ages of 15 to 20 in the 1960s and 1970s, helped drive crime up in those years," Pew said. But the crime rate declined in the early 1980s "as the young boomers got older, then a flare-up by mid-decade in conjunction with a rising street market for crack cocaine, especially in big cities."[9]

By the early 1990s, however, "crack markets withered in part because of lessened demand, and the vibrant national economy made it easier for even low-skilled young people to find jobs rather than get involved in crime. At the same time," Pew said, "a rising number of people ages 30 and older were incarcerated, due in part to stricter laws, which helped restrain violence among this age group."

It is less clear, Pew said, that innovative policing strategies and police crackdowns on use of guns by younger adults played a significant role in reducing crime. "Some researchers have proposed additional explanations as to why crime levels plunged so suddenly, including increased access to abortion and lessened exposure to lead." These were theories, not conclusive findings.

"Crime reductions took place across the country in the 1990s, but since 2000, patterns have varied more by metropolitan area or city," Pew said in the report, issued in 2013.

The Number of Firearms Deaths Compared with Deaths from Other Causes

The number and cause of other deaths in 2016 categorized as injury-related for CDC statistical purposes were:

Drowning: 4,628
Fire: 3,284
Poisoning: 68,995 (This includes deaths resulting from unintentional or intentional overdose of a drug.)

Transportation-related, including accidents involving cars, motorcycles and pedestrians: 42,436

When compared with all causes of death, including disease, homicide was the 16th leading cause in 2015, and guns were used in roughly 73 percent of those deaths, a CDC report said. Far more prevalent, in rank of first through fifth, were heart disease, cancer, chronic lower respiratory diseases, unintentional accidents and stroke.[10]

Suicide came in at number 10. Guns were used in half of all suicides, the report said.

How the Numbers Change by Age Group

As the CDC chart on page 72 shows, different causes of death are more prevalent in certain age groups. In 2015, homicides were listed as a third major cause of death for both the age 15–24 and the 25–34 cohorts. Suicide was second.

By age 35–44, homicides had dropped considerably.

Immediately after Koff posted this FactStack, there were a number of responses from advocates on both sides of the debate asking for additional information behind the numbers:

Was a breakdown by gender available? Could the numbers be compared over a longer period of time? Could some of the terms used be defined with a little more clarity? Participants volleyed back and forth, posting additional articles and websites that backed up their personal points of view. As a result, Koff stepped in as moderator and updated his post. (Editor's note: the updated version is included above.) He addressed the posters with the following:

> I did some more data diving and updated the FactStack with an entire section on long-term trends. I suspect some of you won't be surprised: There was a major dip in gun homicides by 2001, and the rate still is down substantially from levels a decade and two before then . . . [a poster] asked about gender, and I'll answer that here: Of all mass shootings between 1982 and February 2018, 94 percent of the shooters were male, according to Statista. I don't have at my fingertips what the breakdown is if you include all shootings, not just mass shootings, but we can surmise most were by men. Incidentally, homicide victims also tend to be male. 84 percent were in 2016. (Different years for these last two figures because of different sourcing.) If anyone wants to dive into more data on firearms deaths, you can sort numerous ways on this CDC data tool: https://webappa.cdc.gov/sasweb/ncipc/mortrate.html.

Chapter 4

An unfortunate truth that the political and cultural events of recent years have laid bare is that Americans often are tribal by nature, easily and automatically drawn toward voices and opinions that echo their own. Since the 2016 election this phenomenon has become both more readily apparent and, some would argue, more firmly entrenched. The goal of "Guns, An American Conversation" was not to eliminate divides nor to radically alter the opinions of any participants—those would be unfeasible and impractical aims—but rather to offer those in the group strategies for listening openly and to provide tools for keeping difficult conversations civil.

Of course, that wasn't always easy. Within the Facebook group, certain voices dominated from the beginning; some were quick to plant rhetorical flags. That often led to "talking over" other posters, meaning rapid-fire, fact-dense comments that were dubbed by David Preston as "fact bombs." The prevalence of these more frequent, long posts often left quieter voices lurking without posting or retreating to the margins when they felt weary of pushing back.

Meanwhile, moderators worked behind the scenes to help craft Facebook posts, redirect discussions, and call out unproductive behavior. Some of the participants, despite the proddings of moderators, could not or would not change the tone of their comments; because of this, a handful of participants were asked to leave the group. But some of the loudest voices worked hard to try new tactics. Dan Zelenka, a prolific poster and progun advocate, stayed quiet for a bit when asked by moderators to give others a chance to speak.

However, a current within the group mirrored the real world: many times the voices of women and people of color were drowned out. Subsequently, within the first few weeks of the guns conversation, several women requested a women's-only space. Many Spaceship Media projects have been women-only and media partners and the Spaceship team are keenly aware of the divergent challenges of moderating cross-gender vs. single-gender conversations. All group participants tend also to respond differently to guidance from female and male moderators.

But several of the women participating felt like the posts from the male participants were drowning out their own. So after receiving several such requests, the moderators created a women's-only chat subgroup, and posted this question as a conversation starter: "How do you protect yourself against potential danger?"

The query turned into a lively discussion, with more than a hundred comments. Most of the women had a strategy in place. Prevention tactics ranged from walking with a big dog to carrying hair spray or pepper spray, or carrying a firearm. Several women proclaimed the power of their boxing skills.

The conversation also took a deeper turn into why more isn't done by society at large to prevent gendered violence in the first place.

Zekiye Mary Salman said she was drawn to the guns conversation in part because of her interest in ethics and finding common ground. Her background is diverse—half of her family is Middle Eastern Muslim and the other half is Irish Catholic—so she had a natural affinity toward observing and understanding different points of view. In her introduction, she specifically noted that she hoped to learn and explore how education about gun violence could help impact communities. "I wish the resources going into teaching self-defense would go into educating people and supporting people so violence isn't necessary," she said. "I think suggesting women take on this extra work demonstrates the inequity of labor (mental, emotional, and physical) which they should be using to live full lives free from violence. It's another way to uphold the current system and to redirect women's energy by making them responsible for the violence against them."

Alabama gun control advocate Melanie Jeffcoat said the safety debate got her thinking about how the message that women are responsible for men's behavior is apparent, even in middle-school dress codes:

This conversation is making me think about the dress code in my daughter's middle school. The girls had a very strict dress code (no uniforms) and my daughter and others were sent to the office for wearing leggings (even with a long shirt) or shorts above "finger-tip length" and it frustrates me. These girls are pulled out of class and not learning in order to do what—keep the boys' hormones in check? At one point my kid said to me, "Instead of sending the girls home, why not send every boy with an erection to the office?" I died laughing. And the moms of the boys were upset with the moms of the girls. Ugh. Instead of me always reminding my daughter to dress appropriately in order to avoid being raped—more parents need to be talking with their sons about respecting young women. Ok, vent over. ;) My point is, I refuse to live my life looking over my shoulder waiting for impending danger. Hell, a poor woman was sucked out of an airplane window yesterday. Who could have predicted that?? Life is short and I choose to live it with love, light, and laughter. I'm smart and careful and not stupid. But I don't live in a state of fear.

Meredith Glick Brinegar is an Ohio mother and clinical psychologist active in Moms Demand Action, a grassroots movement that advocates for public safety measures to better help prevent gun violence. She explained that she views gun violence as a public health issue:

I truly appreciate what you wrote about somehow putting the onus on women to protect themselves. I share this frustration. Where is the effort to prevent the need to resort to violence in the first place (which is disproportionately done by men)? So this is where I agree. And I feel like I've had many variations of this conversation with female friends and patients, who rail against the idea that we, as women, have to take precautions against sexual assault. Like not walking alone, or not drinking too much. There is a protective and practical part of me that does encourage young women to moderate their drinking. Because I have seen way too many women become victims of sexual assault when alcohol is involved. And yet, why is this women's responsibility? Why can't we be more focused on addressing rape culture, rather than teaching women how to prevent or protect themselves from assault? In this case sexual, but I think the same applies to physical assault. So while I have never carried a gun and don't see this changing, I can understand women who do arm themselves, given that we don't live in a just society and women [are] disproportionately victims of sexual assault and domestic violence. But I don't want that to let us become complacent. That somehow guns are an equalizer. I think we need to keep addressing underlying power differentials among men and women, things like rape culture, and using violence to assert power.

The comments within the women-only posts made it clear that many of the women felt that the gendered double standards they often feel in other parts of their lives did play a role in the broader gun conversation. And like the broader gun conversation, voicing these issues and listening to the viewpoints of others was only one part of the larger conversation and only a step toward bridging divides.

The challenges faced by women were echoed in the larger group as they tackled another difficult-to-address topic: gun violence and race. When participants wrote posts on topics that were difficult, part of the work of moderators was to engage behind the scenes to help them craft their assertions and questions so as best to engage the curiosity and openness of the other group participants. All of this work is part of an ongoing effort by Spaceship Media and its partners to steer people toward less adversarial and combative forms of communication while supporting them in finding paths to openness.

Daniel Boykin II is an African-American gun advocate from Colorado. Boykin was active in his local gun club and a proud member of the National Rifle Association. One of his posts became one of the most contentious of the entire project, reflecting the difficulty of discussing race and guns.

When the gun discussion first started, he had observed: "People genuinely want to have an open dialogue about gun control. They genuinely don't want to argue over it. I think they want to understand other people's views on the issues."

Midway through the project, Boykin entreated members not to make assumptions about black men based on the way that they dress. "It's time to change the perception on black gun owners in America and [in] general black Americans," he wrote, adding, "I want the 'well it's about the way black men dress' narrative to be for naught in justifying racial discrimination."

Boykin went on to explain that at his gun club in Colorado, part of the service he provides is to teach other African Americans about their Second Amendment rights, safety, and self-defense, as well as black gun owner history. Before making his appeal to the group to change the way that they perceive black men, especially those who may be carrying a firearm, he asked members to view a video of a black man shooting in self-defense.

His point on perception was underlined by Brinegar, who related it to rape culture: "As a woman, this makes me think of the 'well look at how she was dressed' excuse for rape and sexual assault. We touched on this some in our women's only post. Clothes never justify rape. Nor fear of black men."

Boykin responded, "Gun violence in black communities will decrease substantially when the jobs come back and when more jobs are created."

In short, Boykin said, poverty leads to violence. "No one needs to rob and steal when they have a job," he said. Boykin presented a theory that if parents, no matter what background, were more actively teaching their children to be more accepting of others, there would be less bullying—and mass shootings.

But he also thought there was another tool that would help pacify the mind: "That's what I believe are some solutions to gun violence," he said, "and maybe a little yoga as an elective in schools across America (which I've been practicing for 4 years myself)," he said, with an added LOL.

Boykin's posts pointed to a central thesis: the high rates of gun violence are related to high rates of racism.

On day seventeen of the project, Boykin and Andy Di-Napoli got into a heated back-and-forth about black men and police officers, a conversation that threatened to go off the rails because of high passions.

The moderators' communication channels were active as they strategized how to work in concert to keep the discussion civil and on track. One relatively new poster, who was deliberately fanning the flames, was asked to leave.

There was a lot of back-and-forth between moderators and Boykin as they tried to find a productive solution. After a discussion with the moderators, Boykin acknowledged that he could have expressed his position in a way that could be more easily heard and processed by others in a more tactful way, and subsequently deleted several sections of some of his comments.

The exchange was described as follows in the morning newsletter: "In one of the most complicated discussions the group has witnessed, Daniel Boykin II of Colorado brought the Black Lives Matter debate into the fore with a multilayered question, paraphrased here: "Historically, blacks have not had the means to protect themselves from white supremacists. Why would black people support gun control measures that would likely lawfully unarm members of the black community?"

The discussion was heated at times, but many found it productive. This is of course not surprising. Spaceship Media's

Eve Pearlman noted this: "The goal is not to create a formal and guarded atmosphere for polite chatter, but rather to support people, day in and day out, in doing the hard work of reflecting not just on their tightly held beliefs but how they engage with others about them in a journalistic space."

Ade Kelly of New Jersey, one of the participants who had traveled to DC for the in-person meeting, had introduced himself to the Facebook group, saying, "This, right here, will change this country for the better. Let's converse!" He stood in the middle of the road on gun control, wanting to preserve the Second Amendment while making sure all kinds of neighborhoods are safe.

He brought this perspective into the discussion about race and guns:

> I believe it is disingenuous to believe race isn't a factor when it comes to gun legislation. We must remember that when the constitution was written African Americans were still considered property. Given that context, gun ownership has always been important and personal to African Americans. I believe it is important for African Americans to exercise that constitutional right. However, there is a need for balance. How can I exercise my rights in a way that is safe? Daniel Boykin is absolutely correct. Systemic racism, whether intentional or plain ignorance, exists. Whenever African Americans exercise the rights written in the constitution, there are forces alive that have tried to suppress what we all

are supposed to be entitled to. I challenge you all to hear us out because this is the reality for many people that look like us.

Moderator Brittany Walker Pettigrew identified a pattern she had noticed in cross-political-lines dialogue: a "storming" phase in which swirling rhetoric takes on a life of its own. But, she said, after a storm she'd often see a bright spot in the conversation.

One such interlude was described in the daily newsletter:

> Jon Godfrey started what became a remarkable conversation by broaching a subject that has had a lot of discussions—the need for anyone handling a gun to know how to do it responsibly—and asking how to get that done. If there were to be mandatory gun safety training, Godfrey asked, "where might be the best venue to present it?"

The ensuing discussion stood out for its specificity of ideas and solutions—and perhaps more so, for its civility, even among those with different ideas.

"I feel like school is an excellent venue because it exposes the masses and doesn't need to be prolonged," Godfrey wrote. "It could also meet a basic requirement for those who need to have a safety standard level of training for responsible ownership. I bet the NRA would even offer instructors. Both my wife and I took our 'hunter's safety course' in our schools. My wife's (great state of Wyoming) was done as part of her science class! I would be interested in both of your thoughts and any other ideas or beliefs you have on this."

Helene Cohen Bludman started the comments off with "Do you think this should happen in high school? Would it be mandatory or voluntary?"

Godfrey replied that first or second grade might be good for an early introduction to such subjects as what to do if you find a gun, but the actual safety course could be in the ninth or tenth grade.

Ade Kelly liked the idea. "Honestly, I'd be open to that. Similar to how drivers ed is mandated at least in my state. If we have a basic understanding of not only gun safety and gun laws both at a federal level and state level."

And John Noel Bartlett recalled that the "Pennsylvania Hunter's Ed course—required for a hunting license—was part of the 7th grade curriculum when our kids were in school. That was a long time ago. I think it made a lot of sense. (Parents could of course opt their kids out.) I think a basic firearms safety course would be valuable. It could potentially decrease the number of accidental shootings."

But he added, "I would rather not have the NRA involved. I will be the first to say they have excellent programs, but the political baggage brought to the table would likely be bothersome to many."

David Preston proposed then that "gun safety could be incorporated into a health class in high school or a hunter safety course in school."

The comments continued, with discussions about the objectives of such a course. Helene Bludman proposed that safe storage be included in the lessons. But she was among those who mentioned a different concern: Can and should guns be part of the public school curriculum? "I'm struggling with this only because it is a giant leap for me from being anti-gun to endorsing gun safety education in schools," she said. "I need to marinate on this a bit."

Others added that they could see parental and political objections. "Honestly, it wouldn't be received well, in my honest opinion," Ade said. "Cities like NYC and states like NJ are ultra left to the point where compromise isn't likely. They advocate for common sense gun law but probably would never go for something as practical as this."

What about making it opt-in?

"The problem with an optional program is that the very people who need the training most would not get it," Dan Zelenka said.

Melanie Jeffcoat wondered, "Are we talking about theoretical training or actual firearms training? Would kids be handling guns? Would teachers?

"I think that sort of conversation is important with kids and parents," she added. "However, I would have a problem with guns being brought into a classroom and kids learning how to handle them. I don't think that is necessary and I think many parents would oppose it."

The conversation continued, with voices across the aisle saying schools had no business teaching students how to use guns.

"Don't expose my kids to gun culture," said Joe Vargo, of Columbus, Ohio. "It's not part of us and we're not part of it."

Guns, An American Conversation

Here is a FactStack by Stephen Koff looking at the results of some other preventive measures against gun violence:

What Was the Assault Weapons Ban?

It was part of the Violent Crime Control and Law Enforcement Act of 1994, passed when President Bill Clinton was in office, that outlawed the manufacture, sale or possession of certain rapid-fire weapons. It lasted for ten years; Congress would not renew it in 2004.

Although some people characterize the bill as a ban on automatic weapons, fully automatic weapons were already largely outlawed years earlier for civilians. The ban covered semiautomatic weapons, or firearms that allow for rapid firing but require a separate pull of the trigger for each shot.

The ban covered eighteen specific firearms plus numerous characteristics and features of military-style guns. Weapons made before the law went into effect could still be owned and resold.

What Kinds of Weapons Were Banned?

Specifically banned were such weapons as Kalashnikovs, UZIs, Beretta Ar70, Colt AR-15s, INTRATEC TEC-9s, TEC-DC9s, and TEC-22s, or copies or duplicates of these. But beyond named weapons, firearms with certain characteristics were also banned. A semiautomatic rifle that could accept a detachable magazine and has at least two of certain features were also banned, with those features including:

- a folding or telescoping stock
- a pistol grip that protrudes conspicuously beneath the action of the weapon
- a bayonet mount
- a flash suppressor or threaded barrel designed to accommodate a flash suppressor
- a grenade launcher

Were There Exceptions or Loopholes?

There were lots of them, according to a number of studies and news reports. For one, assault weapons were used in only 2 percent of gun crimes before the ban. And second, existing weapons were grandfathered, meaning there were an estimated 1.5 million preban assault weapons and 25 million to 50 million large-capacity magazines still in the US.

"Any semi-automatic rifle with a pistol grip and a bayonet mount was an 'assault weapon.'

But a semiautomatic rifle with just a pistol grip might be okay," the *Washington Post* reported. "It was complicated. And its complexity made it easy to evade."

What Did the Ban Accomplish?

The use of assault weapons in the commission of crimes dropped by 17 percent to 72 percent in cities studied—Baltimore, Miami, Milwaukee, Boston, St. Louis, and Anchorage—according to a 2004 analysis for the Justice Department, the last in a series of three reports on the ban. This was largely due to a drop in the use of assault pistols, which were used more commonly than assault rifles in crime. The data showing this drop covered "all or portions of the 1995–2003 post-ban period," the analysis said.[1]

However, the decline was offset throughout at least the late 1990s by the steady or rising use of other guns equipped with large-capacity magazines, the study said. The failure to reduce large-capacity magazines "has likely been due to the immense stock of exempted pre-ban magazines, which has been enhanced by recent imports," it said.

The report concluded it was "premature to make definitive assessments of the ban's impact on gun crime," partly because so many preexisting weapons were exempted.

But another factor was cited: The effects of the ban were "still unfolding and may not be fully felt for several years into the future, particularly if foreign, pre-ban large capacity magazines continue to be imported into the US in large numbers."

Was This the Final Word?

The ban's success or lack thereof remains in debate, partly because of the difficulty of measuring what studies sponsored by the Justice Department set out to assess.

For one, assault weapons were used in such a small share—2 percent—of gun crimes before the ban, Factcheck.org noted, citing the work of Christopher S. Koper, the lead author of the studies for the Justice Department and an associate professor and principal fellow at George Mason University's Center for Evidence-Based Crime Policy. "And second, existing weapons were grandfathered, meaning there were an estimated 1.5 million pre-ban assault weapons and 25 million to 50 million large-capacity magazines still in the US."[2]

The evidence was too limited for any firm

projections, Koper concluded at the time, "but it does suggest that long term restrictions on these guns and magazines could potentially produce at least a small reduction in shootings."

FactCheck.org found that Koper had more to say about the potential effect of an assault weapons ban in an early 2013 presentation: "Consider, for example, at our current level of gun violence, achieving a 1 percent reduction in fatal and non-fatal criminal shootings would prevent approximately 650 shootings annually. . . . And, of course having these sorts of guns, and particularly magazines, less accessible to offenders could make it more difficult for them to commit the sorts of mass shootings that we've seen in recent years."

What Else Has Been Learned about the Ban and Mass Shootings?

The number and rate of mass shootings depend on how mass shootings or massacres are defined, but they are definitely far lower than the rate of gun crimes overall. As of this morning (April 6, 2018), for example, Gun Violence Archive,[3] a nonprofit project that compiles extensive data on gun violence, counted 14,542 gun incidents altogether nationwide so far in 2018.

But the number counted as "mass shooting incidents," involving four or more people shot, was substantially lower, at 58. This is based on information from police blotters, media reports, and other sources.[4]

How Well Did the Assault Weapons Ban Work in Preventing Mass Shootings?

There is debate over this in part because of different definitions. There is no single definition of a mass shooting, the Rand Corporation says. A study of mass shootings involving 6 or more deaths said that in the decade before the ban, there were 19 such incidents, accounting for 155 deaths. During the decade-long ban, the number of incidents fell to 12 and the number of deaths from those mass shootings came to 89. In the decade after the ban expired, the number of such incidents climbed to 34, accounting for 203 deaths.[5]

This is according to Louis Klarevas of the University of Massachusetts Boston, discussing his much-publicized findings with the *Washington Post*. Klarevas is the author of the 2016 book *Rampage Nation: Securing America from Mass Shootings*.

His data suggested that compared with the ten-year period before the ban, the number of gun massacres during the ban period fell by 37 percent, and the number of people dying from gun massacres fell by 43 percent, the *Washington Post* said.[6]

After the ban expired, there was a 183 percent increase in the number of massacres and a 239 percent increase in massacre deaths, Klarevas's data showed.

Is There Another Side to This?

The results change if the parameters of the studies—specifically, the number of victims counted to categorize a "mass shooting" and the actual firearms used—change, says Jon Stokes, founding editor of AllOutdoor.com. He made this point in a *Los Angeles Times* op-ed on March 1, 2018.

If the number of victims counted in a "mass shooting" is reduced to four, as is common in other analyses, instead of the six counted by Klarevas, the 1994 to 2004 drop in mass-shooting fatalities—the efficacy of the assault weapons ban—disappears entirely, Stokes said.[7]

Had Klarevas chosen a "mass shooting" threshold of five fatalities instead of six, then the dramatic pause he notes in mass shootings between 1994 to 1999 would disappear too, Stokes wrote.

For his analysis, Stokes tried to discern which ones would have been covered by the assault weapons ban and which would not. The criteria matter, he said, because a number of "mass shooting" fatalities, if defined as four people, involve single-firing pistols or other guns that were never banned.

All told, he said, there were five mass shootings that took place with "assault weapons"—as defined by the terms of the ban—in the decade before the ban, and three that took place during its tenure. "These numbers are far too small for any sort of statistical inference, especially if you're trying to build a case for banning tens of millions of legally owned rifles," Stokes wrote.

So Is It Settled?

The debate still rages.

In March 2018, the Rand Corporation wrote, "Evidence for the effect of assault weapon bans on mass shootings is inconclusive."[8]

Yet there also have been state-level assault weapons bans, and when factoring those in as well as the federal ban, they have been effective specifically in reducing school shootings—and other gun-control measures have not been, said Mark Gius, an economics professor at Quinnipiac University, in 2017 in the journal *Applied Economic Letters.*[9]

He wrote that "assault weapons bans reduced the number of school shooting victims by 54.4 percent. All other gun control laws (concealed carry laws, private sale background checks, and federal dealer background checks) had no statistically significant effects on school shootings."

This was partly noteworthy because Gius said in previous research that assault weapons bans had no significant effect on the much larger subset of state-level murder rates. Again, relatively few murders are committed using assault weapons compared with those using other guns, and Gius was specifically addressing school shootings in this analysis.[10]

Chapter 5

As the guns conversation came into the final few days, moderators and participants shared closing posts touching on what they had learned from engaging with other people. Over the course of the month, the discussions that took place demonstrated that any conversation about guns in general is about many other topics, including about safety, family, culture, and about the fundamental rights of Americans. A conversation about guns is never just about guns.

Although the closing posts varied in length and structure, collectively they echoed a hopefulness. While many of the participants noted their views on guns and gun control hadn't changed, they noted that they had become more understanding of the other side, and that being an active part of the conversation project would spur many of them to continue actively listening and carrying on holding constructive conversations in their communities.

To kick off the farewell posts, Michelle Holmes shared a reflection that touched on the progress the group had made:

> Hello, all. The time has come to look toward the horizon.
>
> This group, "Guns, an American Conversation," will close next Friday, May 4, 2018, at noon. First things first: it has been a real adventure and pleasure, challenging and edifying, to host you all.
>
> It has been an honor to witness your very difficult undertaking, which is to engage in an ongoing, civil online conversation (on Facebook, no less!), with people who hold very different views about guns, gun rights, and gun safety. From our perspective, you—those who commented a lot and those who mostly listened— have stayed in the room, and are doing what you can to talk to and understand people with whom you disagree.
>
> No, you have not and likely will not reach a consensus on what gun laws should be, whether the Second Amendment needs altering, or most other issues to do with firearms. But that was in no way the point! Some of you have, at times, edged into areas of agreement on topics including waiting periods, red flag warnings, and background checks— which is worth remembering.

Far more importantly, though, are your efforts to understand the perceptions, feelings and points of view of other people. We look forward to watching that continue in our last week together—it's one of the things that makes those so worthwhile. Enjoy your last week together!

Love, your whole mods and journos team.

Lavin then highlighted reflections from some of the people who had traveled to DC in response to the question "What I want others to understand about my position." The responses demonstrated the diversity of backgrounds, feelings, and expectations of members—those in the room and the collective online Facebook group:

- I want people to understand that I am a gun owner and that I am willing to listen and discuss ideas.
- I am not looking to take your guns away from you as long as you legally possess them.
- I want to feel more understood about my concern for the strong emotional bond that many Americans have with firearms.
- I really want people to understand that I am conservative, I do believe we need to do something to end all the shootings.
- Mental health used to be part of background checks.

- I want people to understand that a desire for gun control is a reasonable and valid desire in this age and time.
- Our gun culture makes America more of a dangerous place. It does not make America a safer place. This scares me.
- Effective and more regulations will not "take away your rights" or impede your choice to own guns.
- I want others to understand that I am not too young to understand this issue. All I want is to come home at the end of the school day.
- There's a middle ground if we all bend some.
- I would like people to understand that criminals don't follow laws, only law-abiding citizens do.
- I want people to understand most is my desire to solve school shootings and gun crime is a passion.
- I want people to understand that I feel like I'm fighting for my right to be alive.
- As a law-abiding gun owner, I am not a danger to you.
- I don't want to take any guns from any law abiding citizens, but I need to feel safe.
- I really want people to understand that I want to find a way to reduce gun deaths and injuries.
- I want to keep guns out of the hands of the wrong people . . . not just criminals, people in crisis, children and those who would misuse them.

- To NOT look at my perspective as coming from a minority, but come from a human being.

It was clear that these were voices that wanted to be heard—voices with opinions that were reflective of the diversity of the country.

Moderator Brittany Walker Pettigrew, who came to the conversation having been a participant in a prior Spaceship Media project, remarked on the positivity she felt hearing the different opinions in the group, and the hope that it held for the future:

> It has been my honor to serve with all of you. I have been humbled by the team of moderators and journalists and all of you! I have enjoyed learning from all of you and gained deeper understanding. I really appreciate the focus on Civil Rights. . . . I have never been in such a diverse group that was so concerned about my civil rights before! I wish you all well . . . and keep talking! Spread the gospel of listening! Be well.

Melanie Jeffcoat, the Alabama mom and committed gun-control advocate, reflected on her experience both in DC and in the Facebook group:

> I was raised by parents who taught us (through example) that if you don't go change the world for the better, who will? Change is hard. We cannot agree on which changes are good because we all look at

progress through the lens God and life has given us. We all come with our stories (which is really just a nice way to say baggage) and our perspectives. We can learn and we can grow, evolve, even completely change our minds on things, but we will never shake loose from our core. I was a little concerned about coming to DC. Although I am passionate about this issue, I do not like confrontation as it is generally fruitless and unproductive at best and hurtful at worst. After talking with John Sarrouf and being reassured that although there were 20 others coming to DC. they all were coming with open minds and a willingness to discuss this issue, I boarded the plane for the adventure of a lifetime. That weekend was a life-changer for me. I bonded deeply with my fellow Americans—people I otherwise would have gone a lifetime without ever meeting. We shared, cried, laughed and grew to respect and value each other. We learned how to listen with empathy and lead with curiosity. The move into the Facebook group was challenging and a bit overwhelming. But it was fascinating to see how some people embraced this kinder, gentler platform and others struggled to let go of what I called "old Facebook." My hope is that we all can take this kind of deep, thoughtful communication into our own personal social media outlets. Always keep in mind that the person you are disagreeing with has a story of their own and that perhaps it might change the course if you ask about it. For me, I will continue to work to reduce the number of gun deaths in my beautiful city of Birmingham. I will engage with people who may differ [from] me politically but want to live in a safer country. When we want the same thing, and I believe all Americans do, we can find ways to arrive at that destination together. Thank you to John and Parisa Parsa for the incredible opportunity and a HUGE shout-out to all of the moderators who kept 130 of us on track for a month. No small task. To my dear DC friends, I'll catch ya on the 20. Now that I finally made the cut.

Jeffcoat's poignant note touched on the humanity that all the participants in the group shared—that despite their differing viewpoints, that all wanted the same thing: to live their lives safely and happily.

Adrian Moy echoed the feeling of unity that Jeffcoat and others touched on in their posts, and provided a summary of what he found to be the key points of the discussion:

A farewell post . . . this month has gone by quickly. First, I am grateful to be one of the "chosen" for the Washington group. Meeting face to face with the journalists, the facilitators, and the other chosen few was priceless. This was clearly a case where the whole was greater than the sum of the parts. Their stories and perspectives on life will live within me long after this forum has concluded.

A quick shout-out to Daniel Kennamore from Alabama, who I spoke with one on one. This Oregon liberal (who happens to be a gun owner) and I were able to talk for quite some time on some pragmatic approaches that just might move this process forward. A bullet point summary, sure to rile up both the "gun rights" and "ban the guns" groups:

- Registration for legal guns
- New, improved, effective background checks (NICS)
- "Grandfather" rights for vintage and heirloom guns
- Licensing and training for concealed and open carry
- No ban on semi-automatic pistols or long guns
- Acknowledge that AR-15 is NOT an assault rifle
- Enforce gun laws to reduce number of illegal guns
- Red flag laws—with some teeth
- Violent offender: Guns taken while case is adjudicated
- Examples: Credible threats, assaults, domestic violence, stalking, road rage, DUI, robbery, burglary, drug offenses
- Mental health crisis intervention (suicide, self-harm, or harm to others)
- More study on underlying causes of violence in all forms

- Educational and vocational opportunities for at-risk youth
- Prison reform/earn a second chance to be a productive member of society

Clearly, even in a quick and incomplete summary, these issues are complex. The solutions will not come from the lunatic fringe or the politicians beholden to K Street lobbyists and PACs. We need to look at a bigger picture, and ask who we are as a people, who we want to become, and how we define our own American Dream.

Then look even deeper, and realize we are all part of one human species, with our brief history largely shaped by violence, war, injustice, and brutality. In a span of roughly 500 years, the weapons of war have quickly evolved from rocks, spears, swords and arrows to the array of deadly weapons in our hands today, from the guns we are concerned about in this forum, up to and including ballistic missiles with thermonuclear warheads that could bring about our quick and final annihilation. The current reality is, none of these weapons are going away anytime soon, and no one is willing to disarm unilaterally, either on the micro or the macro scale. The rapid development of technology, for good and evil, has upset our evolutionary clock, and we will not solve the crises we face now or in the future by continuing to do what we have done in the past. I hope that we and future generations of humans have the desire and the courage to seek and implement pragmatic and practical solutions to the intractable problems we face, and thereby earn the opportunity to further evolve. If we are lucky, we might even learn to let bygones be bygones, and one day live together in peace and prosperity on our healthy and beautiful planet.

I thank all the participants in this forum for reminding me, once again, that our destiny is shared, and it is up to us to figure that out. Live long and prosper. . . .

The thread of hope and unity continued in Ade Kelly's closing post. A podcaster from New Jersey who was open to gun-control reform, Kelly specifically noted the connections that he felt both in DC and in the Facebook group:

When I initially saw the post to join this group and travel down to Washington, DC, I knew this was bigger than myself. I knew I had to be open-minded and listen twice as much as I spoke.

My position was clear in my eyes, preserve the Second Amendment while also keeping Americans from all over safe. Safe in inner cities like I grew up in, safe in suburban towns, and safe in rural areas as well. But I had no idea how to get there. I also must admit prior to DC I had no understanding of why someone needed an AR-15.

So in DC I listened, I listened to people on my left and my right. DC gave me clarity of people on all sides, it gave me friendships with some fine Americans, and it gave me hope. We left DC knowing that we all agreed on the need for safety in this country and that social media needs some humanity. We all left DC connected. I must say due to leaning liberal on many issues, I could not have predicted having friends on the other side of me politically, but we all need that.

What I got out of this Facebook group was some more hope. We can communicate effectively on social media. I think some in this group were a little intimidated when racial issues were brought up. However, it played a huge part in this country. I can't turn the hue of my skin off. I wish more of you all actually challenged yourselves to actually participate more openly for that aspect of the conversation. But this has brought me hope nonetheless. I plan on using what we started here and spilling that into my community. Don't be surprises [*sic*] if you see my face on TV or on a clip referencing this as a pivotal moment in bringing us all closer together. (For those outside of DC I do have political aspirations down the line, so please open the [door] and sign my petitions when I come knocking lol)

Thank you All! Huge shout-out to the moderators and all the parties involved in facilitating this here. And to the DC crew! If anyone in the NJ/NY area would like to grab a drink, lunch, coffee, join my podcast, please hit me up anytime.

Although each of the closing posts ended the participant's discussion on a positive note, not all of the members felt changed by the shared experience. Kris Eggert, the gun control advocate from Cleveland, kept her post brief, thanking the group and noting that she'd be continuing her activist work in her community.

> Thanks for the opportunity to be part of this group. For those who are actively involved in gun control efforts, you encouraged me. Check out our work on our God Before Guns FB page. And to those who resist any changes whatsoever, you make me even more determined. May peace and justice prevail.

Daniel Boykin, the gun advocate whose thoughts on race and firearms set off some of the project's most thoughtful and intense moments, penned perhaps one of the most notable closing posts:

> As one of the original 21 people on this project, I learned a lot more than I expected to learn from it, especially from the newer 130 people (who joined the Facebook after the DC weekend.)
> Thus some of the lessons that I learned from this have implemented into the policy of one of the

Facebook gun groups created by the Oregon Gun Club—NAAGA, "Black Gun Owners-Black America." Those strategies include how to genuinely listen to and process the ideologies of those who oppose you, how to get your point across without insulting those who oppose your beliefs and a few more reasons. Now, we may not ever agree on our views but I think that a few of us, like myself, have had a mind-changing experiences [*sic*] with this project.

By joining "Guns, An American Conversation," Boykin had learned how to actively listen to the other side and was implementing what he learned in his community. In Boykin's case, the needle had moved.

Although her personal point of view didn't change, Helene Cohen Bludman, the Pennsylvania grandmother, remarked that she had learned to more actively listen through her participation in the Facebook group.

Happy Friday! It is my turn to express my gratitude for being chosen to participate in this group. I have tried to listen to all views and appreciate those who did the same for me. My position on guns has not changed but my ability to acknowledge alternate viewpoints has. Thank you especially to the mods for all their dedication. Onward!

And in demonstrating how her participation in the group made her more aware of the nuances of language that surround guns, Bludman posted: "I might have chosen anti–gun activist before but now it is anti-gun violence activist."

Retired army master sergeant and police chief Jon Godfrey's final post really drove the message of the conversation home:

The time has come for me to end my participation in this great event. So here is my "What I've learned while part of 'Guns, An American Conversation.'" I've learned and rededicated myself to the power of real conversation thanks to John & Parisa at Essential Partners. I've learned that with conversation and curiosity about the other side we can bridge some gaps, but it's not likely to change anyone's mind. I've learned that the social media has taken the civility out of dialog and we must guard against that and look for ways to make a human connection. I've learned that race relations still has a big divide and that as far as many minorities are concerned, they need to define and tell their story, not someone else, and that is rightfully so.

I've confirmed that the mental health portion of gun violence is being denied by much of the mental health community, even though 66% of all gun violence is suicides, and knowing what I already experienced, I'm not surprised. I've learned that the media tries to be balanced and unbiased, even when they each may have personal liberal or conservative roots, they try every day. They sometimes fail, however, in this monthlong event, they have always come right back and hit that wall with a moderate investigative approach.

And lastly, I have learned what I probably always knew. I learned that people are always the key. The people of this conversation and in particular the original legacy members of the DC group of 21 are some of the finest people I have ever had the pleasure of being associated with. I have experienced shared hardships with men and women in combat, and although this is nowhere near that level, I will remember many of you in a very similar way.

And with some final closeouts, the monthlong "Guns, An American Conversation" officially ended on May 4, 2018. In total, there had been close to 15,000 posts from the 150 participants. Although some may have worried that the group hadn't come up with concrete solutions, nearly all participants and moderators marveled at the civility and decency that was threaded through even the most heated discussions. That civil discussion was able to—for the most part—reign supreme, and that even those at the opposite ends of the political spectrum were able to actively listen to the other side, was a sign of hope, a step in the right direction. If 150 Americans—representative of a diversity of thought, experience, geography, age, and gender—could choose to come together and work to hear each other out, maybe the rest of the country could as well.

Afterword

I am writing this piece at the beginning of April 2020, during what looks to be the beginning of a long and difficult chapter in global history—one that will be defined in great part by the various and wide-ranging impacts of Covid-19.

In this context, as we are facing such a demanding challenge, one that is a threat to our health and well-being on all levels, our ability to understand that we are all in it together is more important than ever. Every day, more than ever, we are all recognizing that what we do, where we go, how we live, and who we touch intimately impact the rest of the humans with whom we share this globe. This is true for me, and you, and all of us. It is a lesson worth learning.

Spaceship's work of recognizing, building on, and holding true to an understanding of our shared fate matters more than ever. It brings me deep joy to continue to be a part of a movement that is doing the work of creating, tending to, and replicating authentic and respectful conversations about polarizing topics. It is hopeful that so many recognize the value and importance of these sorts of efforts.

There are many groups that also have been mediating and moderating conversations about difficult issues for decades, helping people to slow down, engage, listen, and understand one another. These organizations are too multitudinous to mention, but you can find them in your community. As a starting place, check out the Bridge Alliance, the Listen First Project, or the National Center for Dialogue and Deliberation.

And as journalism continues to ride the rapidly changing financial, cultural, and technological landscape, many organizations have risen to find different ways to engage with their communities around polarizing issues and new ways to get people the information they need to stay as safe and aware as possible. I find all of this progress tremendously heartening, and I have confidence in our collective ability to do the work we need to respond humanely and holistically to our evolution in this global, digital world.

A quick reminder: in my work, both online and off, I often hear things like this constantly: "But he did X, said Y, acted in Z way, so I am doing, saying it back." Or: "He called my candidate a name, so I am doing the same to his." Now, if our children did this, most of us would say something along the lines of, "Yes, he did that, but don't respond in kind." Another's bad behavior doesn't justify your own. Time after time, we all encounter these types of situations. So why is the Golden Rule so profoundly difficult? Why are we so quick to create waivers for ourselves? And why are we so blind to our own behavior when we do create them?

As various sages have noted, we can't control others, we can only control ourselves. We are responsible for our words, our behavior. Try to remember this when you are angry or triggered. Ask yourself, *What am I missing? What am I not understanding? How might this person have some perspective or ideas that I can learn from? How is my own bias, my own experience, my own habits, my own life circumstances keeping me from seeing this clearly? How can I be kinder, gentler, more part of the solution?*

I recognize that this is all easier said than done. After all, if all this were easy, we would have done it already. If it were easy, the *Guns* conversation would not have required a team of moderators working around the clock to support and hold people as they did this difficult work. If talking to others with differing views were easy, it would be as simple as saying, "Let's all talk, and suddenly we will see eye to eye and get along." But it isn't easy or simple or straightforward, but it gets better in the trying. So try we must. We must work to understand and recognize our shared humanity, even when we disagree and disagree profoundly. We must.

Eve Pearlman,
cofounder of Spaceship Media

Acknowledgments

Spaceship Media's work has been supported by dozens, if not hundreds, of kind, generous, and thoughtful people, new professional friends, family members, loyal old friends. These are people who gave their support, monetary and technical, spiritual and emotional, in myriad ways and on myriad platforms.

We've been lucky also to work across professional disciplines—journalism, mediation, technology, psychology, neuroscience, sociology—and draw on the wisdom of those who've been doing good work for decades, as well as those who come to this work of bridging divides post-2016.

We are grateful to everyone else who is working to reform journalism to rethink and repattern public communications, from vocal public advocates, to people working tenaciously in the trenches.

Acknowledgments

Spaceship Media would not ever have been born, however, without the day-in and day-out kitchen-table wisdom of two teens, Oliver and Talia. It is those young adults, like their engaged and thoughtful peers around them, who show all of us, every day, paths to better futures. There is also another, somewhat younger person, Alexandra Marie, who like many children brings joy and honesty and hopefulness wherever she goes. They give hope, and for them we must insist on being hopeful.

Additional Resources

Guns One-on-One Convo Guide

Person to Person: Talking about Guns

Introduction

This guide will help prepare you to speak about what is most important to you in ways that can be heard, and to hear others' concerns and passions with new empathy and understanding— even and *especially* if you continue to disagree.

The guide offers a step-by-step approach to inviting another person—someone whose perspectives differ from your own—into a conversation in which:

- You agree to set aside the desire to persuade the other and instead focus on developing a better understanding of each other's perspectives, and the hopes, fears, and values that underlie them;

- You agree to be curious and to avoid the pattern of attack-and-defend; and
- You choose to ask questions and move beyond stereotypes and assumptions.

The Challenge: Why Is This Conversation So Difficult?

Talking about guns in America is challenging in this political climate because when we talk about guns, we express what we really care about—our hopes, our values, and our deepest concerns.

It's about our children's education, or our religious commitments, or our sense of justice, or the future of the planet, or our standing in the world, or our personal sense of safety and health—or *all* of the above. That's no small matter. It's no wonder that when we talk about guns, things can get difficult—because we are really talking about the things we hold most dearly.

Someone challenging our hopes or belittling our fears can put us instantly on the defensive, and provoke us to attack or shut down, which in turn provoke the other person to attack or shut down. And then where are we? Where we are now: divided.

But it doesn't have to be this way. This guide is here to help.

Why Bother? Why Is It So Important? What's at Stake?

Most of us have at least one important relationship that has either been strained by painful conversations about political differences or silenced due to fear that it could get ugly. The options seem to be: bring it up and fight about it, or avoid the conversation—and sometimes the person—altogether. Both options limit who we can be together with as friends or family, and both limit what we can accomplish in our communities.

What alternatives are there?

You can let media pundits and campaign strategists tell you that polarization is inevitable and hopeless. OR you can consider reaching out and taking a journey with someone who believes differently than you.

With some tools to support your best intentions, you can actually learn about what motivates other people and understand how they've come to believe the way they do.

Connecting across our differences is both possible and necessary.

How to Start

Are you ready?
Are they?

Ask yourself:

- Why do I want to connect? What do I want to learn?

- Am I ready to resist the strong pull toward getting angry or frustrated?
- Is just trying to understand each other enough, or will I feel the need to persuade them to concede certain points?

What can you do to prepare yourself to listen without interrupting, and to speak with care?

**Your conversation is most
likely to go well if you:**

- Share the same hopes for the conversation;
- Have some good agreements about how to talk and work together; and
- Have some good questions to start you off.

Choosing Your Spots

Are the time and place right for a good conversation?

Do you need a private place? Can you find enough time, and free yourself from distractions? Where is the place that brings out the best in you? Might a good cup of coffee or tea help?

Find a pressure-free time for both of you, and set yourself up in a comfortable spot as if you were entertaining someone who is already a friend.

Extending the Invitation

To invite the kind of conversation you want to have, be clear about the purposes.

Try this:

> "I really want to be able to talk about this with you. Do you think we can have an honest conversation about this—not just an argument? Can we try to hang in there and listen even when one of us says something the other really doesn't understand?"

If they say no, then you have to accept that. But it's worth a try anyway!

Agreeing on How to Talk

Having a good conversation can be a lot like driving: it's amazing how people can navigate around each other if they have a few rules of the road.

Create Some Agreements to Follow So That You Can Listen with Resilience. Make Them Simple and Easy to Remember.

Try this:

> "It's going to help me bring my best self if we can agree to three simple things. Let's

- **share the time:** let's not interrupt each other, and be sure neither person goes on too long.
- **speak for ourselves:** let's speak from our personal experiences vs. representing or defending entire political parties.
- **respect each other's differences:** by not being too critical or dismissive; aiming simply to understand and not to persuade each other."

Ask each other: "Do these work? Is there anything we need to add?" Customize your agreements to your conversation.* The only rule is that all parties must agree for the agreements to live up to their name!

Start with a Good Question

If you ask a yes-or-no question, you will get a yes-or-no answer.

But if you ask a question that invites people to talk about what is important to them, or what issues are most complex to them, you will be halfway to a productive and civil conversation.

Introductions:

Since you probably have not talked with your conversation partner before, start with a question that helps you get to know

· · · · · · · · ·

* In relationships where these conversations have proven to be difficult in the past, you may need more structure. In our dialogue work around the most difficult issues, we sometimes have people take turns speaking for three minutes and ask them to hold to that limit—it's easier to listen to someone intently when you know they aren't going to go on and on and on . . .

each other. We like introductory questions that get us out of the usual rut of identifying ourselves by profession or status and into learning unexpected stories. Try one of these:

- Tell a story about the significance of your name. What do you know about what it means or how it was chosen? What does it mean to you?
- Think about a wise person in your life who has influenced you (and specifically, your desire to be part of a conversation like this one). Who is it, and how did they influence you?
- What is your favorite childhood memory and why?

Choose the same question for both of you to respond to, then take a couple of minutes in silence to think about what you want to say. Offer your answers in just a couple of minutes, being sure to share the time.

Feel free to ask follow-up questions or take time to note points of commonality or surprises as you continue to talk. Just try not to interrupt!

Getting into the Conversation about Guns

Going deeper into conversation, you will want to turn to more topical questions.

Be sure it's not an interview, with one person asking all the questions. Take turns on the same questions by taking a moment to think about your responses before either of you shares. This will make it possible for you to truly listen to each other, rather than "listening" while actually trying to come up with what you want to say next.

Try these questions:

- What is it in your life experience that has led you to believe the things you believe about guns?
- What hopes, concerns, and values do you have that underlie your beliefs?
- What is at the heart of your beliefs about guns?

Once you have been able to talk about the things you really believe in and care about, you may be more willing to talk about more complex and difficult topics. Try:

- In what ways have you felt out of step with the party/groups you generally support on this issue; or, in what ways do those groups not fully reflect what's important to you?
- What aspects of the other party or advocacy groups do you admire—or at least see as reasonable counterbalances to the groups you generally support?

One important possibility is for someone to define him/herself and step away from stereotypes they feel are placed on them. Try:

- During debates or in the news, what are the ways that you feel your values and perspectives are stereotyped by the "other side"?
- What about who you are and what you care

about makes those stereotypes especially frustrating or painful?

- Are there some stereotypes about you that you feel are *somewhat* deserved—even if they are not fully true?

Getting Back on Track

Bringing it back if/when the conversation has been hijacked, sidetracked, and/or lost in translation.

When things get really tough or the disagreement is profound (and there is a good chance that will happen), remember your purpose is to understand, *not* persuade.

Tune in: Are you really listening? Are you listening to understand or to find fault? When you hear something that just doesn't make any sense to you or that you really disagree with, make sure you have heard the person and let them know you are trying to understand. Try this:

"Let me make sure I understand what you mean. You are saying that this is important to you because _____ and that you really wish _____. Is that right?"

Get curious: The times when you are most frustrated are when you have to get most curious. First, get curious about yourself—*Why is this so difficult for me?* And then be curious about your conversation partner or partners. Use this simple formula:

- **Repeat** what you heard, naming what you hear is most important to them.

- **Name** what is most important for you.
- **Ask** an honest question about how they came to their beliefs or why this is so important to them. Or ask how they can hold one belief and also another seemingly competing belief.

Need to Cool Down? Time for a Break.

It's one of those things we learned in kindergarten, right? Now we know it takes about twenty minutes for the chemicals in our body to get back to normal when we have gotten really upset. If this happens to you but you want to continue the conversation, name your desire to continue and suggest a short break.

Dos, Don't Dos, and Things to Avoid

There are classic pitfalls to good conversation, as well as proven alternatives that will help the conversation be constructive and rewarding to you and your partner or partners.

Keep the following suggestions in mind, especially at moments when you feel yourself becoming triggered or reactive.

Things to avoid:

- Belittling other people's hopes or fears—it only invites the same in response.
- Relying too much on statistics to "win the argument." Statistics and facts are important to explain *why* you have come to the conclusion you have, but there is a good chance that some-

one who believes something differently has their own set of statistics to back it up.

- Generalizing about "people like you." Each one of us is an individual, and it only pushes people farther away when we clump people together.

DON'T:	DO:
Tell your conversation partner they are "wrong."	Ask them what value led them to their claim.
Ask how they "could ever believe that."	Ask when/how that belief first started for them.
Interrupt your conversation partner or partners while they are speaking.	Give them a moment to make sure they've said what they meant to say.
Counter them with "yeah, but what about . . ."	Try "Huh, interesting. Can you tell me more?"
Assume you know their motives.	Ask about their goals and their hopes.
Blame them for your anger or frustration.	Explain your frustration, and own it.

Always Appreciate Your Partner or Partners!

At the end of your conversation together, always take time to name what you have learned from one another, and thank your partner or partners for the experience of a new kind of conversation.

Credits and more information:

Adapted from Essential Partners' *Reaching Across the Divide* guide to red-blue conversations, by Maggie Herzig and John Sarrouf (copyright © 2016 Essential Partners, Inc.)

Copyright © 2018, Essential Partners, Inc.

About us: Essential Partners has worked for more than twenty-seven years to facilitate conversations and equip people to communicate using Reflective Structured Dialogue (RSD), a method that relies on preparation, structure, questions, facilitation, and reflection to enable people to harness their capacity to have the conversations they need to have.

Advancing the work of the Public Conversations Project

Who Owns Guns?

*The Demography of
Gun Ownership*

By Stephen Koff

Americans have "a deep history and a complex relationship with guns," write Ruth Igielnik and Anna Brown[1] of the Pew Research Center. Our attitudes toward guns can reflect personal and cultural experiences, perceptions of ourselves and others, and more.[2]

But the basic question of who owns guns is easier to answer, in part because the Pew Research Center has done extensive polling over recent years. The results are not only revealing but also can help toward understanding differences in gun-ownership beliefs.

Here are some of the findings on ownership from respondents who participated in Pew's March and April 2017 survey panels, involving 3,930 respondents nationwide.[3]

Guns in Households

Thirty percent of American adults say they currently own a gun, and another 11 percent say they don't personally own a gun but live with someone who does. That puts the share of gun-owning households in the United States at 42 percent. (Rounding accounts for the slight math difference.)

Among those who don't currently own a gun, 52 percent of adults say they could see themselves owning one in the future, and 71 percent who owned one in the past could see owning another.

Men, Women, and Race

"Gun ownership is more common among men than women, and white men are particularly likely to be gun owners," Pew says. Thirty-nine percent of men said they personally own a gun, compared with 22 percent of women.

By race:

- Thirty-six percent of whites reported that they are gun owners.
- Twenty-four percent of blacks in the poll said they own a gun.
- Fifteen percent of Hispanics say they own a gun.

Racial identities come from parameters in the 2015 Census Bureau's American Community Survey. Says the Census Bureau, "These standards generally reflect a social definition of race and ethnicity recognized in this country, and they do not conform to any biological, anthropological, or genetic criteria."[4]

Look how the numbers change when you consider total household gun ownership.

- Forty-nine percent of white respondents said someone in their household owns a gun.
- The share of gun ownership by household drops to 32 percent for black respondents.
- The household gun ownership rate is 21 percent for Hispanic respondents.

Rural, Urban, Suburban

Forty-six percent of participants who live in rural parts of the country said they own a gun, and the share in rural areas grows to 58 percent when counting gun-owning households (e.g., someone else in the home owns a gun).

In other words, rural residents are more likely than not to have a gun in the household.

That compares with 28 percent of adults who live in suburbs owning a gun. But the suburban share of gun ownership grows to 41 percent when it includes others in the household.

Urban residents say they have fewer guns: 19 percent of the adults polled. The share grows to 29 percent when guns in the household, and not just those owned by the individual respondents, are included.

North and South

Northeasterners are the least likely Americans to own a gun. Here is gun ownership by region:

- Northeast: 16 percent (27 percent if measured by guns in household)
- South: 36 percent (45 percent if measured by guns in household)
- Midwest: 32 percent (44 percent if measured by guns in household)
- West: 31 percent (46 percent if measured by guns in household)

Types of Guns

Among owners with only one gun, handguns are the most common, with 62 percent saying this is what they own. That's followed by 22 percent who own a rifle and 16 percent who own a shotgun.

But among all gun owners, more than one firearm is more common. Among owners with more than one gun, 72 percent own a handgun or pistol, while 62 percent own a rifle and 54 percent own a shotgun.

"Men are particularly likely to own multiple guns: About three-quarters of male gun owners (74 percent) say they own two or more guns, compared with 53 percent of female gun owners," Pew says. "This reflects, in part, the fact that men who own guns are more likely than their female counterparts to have more than one reason for doing so. Still, even after controlling for the number of reasons they own a gun, male gun owners remain more likely than their female counterparts to own multiple guns."

Education Levels and Gun Ownership

Pew's polling shows that gun ownership rates are somewhat lower among people with a college education. Nevertheless, the numbers show that 25 percent of people with at least a bachelor's degree own a gun.

- High school education or less: 31 percent
- Some college: 34 percent
- Bachelor's degree or higher: 25 percent

This changes, however, when only white respondents are counted; theirs was the only group showing this kind of difference. For white respondents:

- High school diploma or less: 40 percent
- Some college: 42 percent
- Bachelor's degree or higher: 26 percent

Pew also polled on attitudes and perceptions, experiences, views on gun safety, and views on gun regulation. You can access it at pewresearch.org.[5] The margin of error in its polling on guns was plus or minus 2.8 percentage points. The full methodology is available online.[6]

Accidental Gun Deaths

By John Counts

"There are thousands of accidental shootings each year, including about 600 fatalities," according to *The Gun Debate: What Everyone Needs to Know* by Philip J. Cook and Kristin A. Goss.

From a *Los Angeles Times* story, "Amid rising gun violence, accidental shootings have plummeted. Why?" dated January 1, 2018: "There were 489 people killed in unintentional shootings in the US in 2015, the most recent year for which data is available. That was down from 824 deaths in 1999, according to the Centers for Disease Control and Prevention. Taking into account population growth over that time, the rate fell 48%."[7]

A CDC report has the 2015 number (489) cited in the *LA Times* story. It's on page 33 and has it broken down by age groups. Coincidentally, it's right next to accidental drownings (3,602 in 2015). Broken down by age groups, accidental discharge of firearms in 2015 accounted for 1 death of a baby under one, 25 children ages 1–4, 22 children ages 4–15, 121 people ages 15–21, 79 people ages 22–34, 59 people ages 35–45, 57 people ages 45–54, 55 people ages 55–64, 45 people ages 65–74, 18 people ages 75–84, and 7 people ages 85 and over.[8]

The number for 2015 seems to be the most recent out there. The Pew Research Center, which also got their data from the CDC, had a report from five years earlier: "In 2010, there were 31,672 deaths in the US from firearm injuries, mainly through suicide (19,392) and homicide (11,078), according to CDC compilation of data from death certificates. The remaining firearm deaths were attributed to accidents, shootings by police and unknown causes." That's 1,202 firearm deaths in 2010 that weren't suicides or homicides.[9]

Additional Information about Dialogue Journalism

What Is Dialogue Journalism?

Dialogue Journalism is a method for convening and supporting fact-based conversations between people on opposite sides of polarizing social and political fractures. It is a process for engaging divided communities deeply and connecting them with the newsrooms and journalists who serve them. Dialogue Journalism creates a new news cycle, one that starts from the questions and issues that divided communities are discussing. Dialogue Journalism puts community at the heart of journalistic practice.

Additional Resources

Eve Pearlman, Spaceship Media CEO and Cofounder, *Tiny Spark* Podcast: "Going to the heart of divides, bringing communities together in dialogue across differences, supporting those conversations with fact, telling stories about those conversations and about the issues and topics that arise from them—this is the work of Dialogue Journalism."

Dialogue Journalism was created with the intention of going to the heart of social and political divides. By going to places of friction in society, as journalists always have, but once there doing something different: building respectful, fact-based conversations between regular people about the issues that matter deeply to all of us as a society. We put the core tools of our journalistic craft directly in service to the divided communities we help build. At its most basic, Dialogue Journalism is a seven-step method for identifying divides and then creating sustained, nurtured, and moderated conversations between groups of people who have not been communicating or who have not been communicating effectively.

Michelle Holmes, VP Content, Alabama Media Group: "Spaceship Media offers a potent balm for alienation, cynicism, distrust, and fear. Their model has shown how divided people can come together to grapple with tough questions and emerge with new insight."

Eve Pearlman, *Resistance Dashboard* Podcast: "We were watching the increasing polarization and dysfunction in our public spaces, in and around journalism and on social media. We knew we wanted to go right to where there was trouble and difficulty, but we wanted to go there to support those situations with information and with opportunities for communication. . . .

This comes from our core impulses to listen first and to engage and to support. That was the beginning of Spaceship Media."

Key Takeaways of Dialogue Journalism

- Dialogue Journalism is a method developed by Spaceship Media that can be utilized by newsrooms to bridge divides.
- Dialogue Journalism projects start by identifying divided communities, places where people are not communicating or not communicating productively, and then brings them into dialogue for respectful, fact-supported conversations.
- Dialogue Journalism reconfigures the reporting process, with reporters providing information directly to the divided communities they serve.
- Dialogue Journalism projects are supported by original reporting, what we call FactStacks: nonnarrative compendiums of facts and figures created directly in response to the issues and topics that people are discussing.

Further Reading

"Assault or Homicide." National Center for Health Statistics, Centers for Disease Control and Prevention, n.d. https://www.cdc.gov/nchs /fastats/homicide.htm?fbclid=IwAR2li71xERGJcQ5SdGqwhibz8fU OMNN8ZlEaKVrDB-HBxPpzNXfTYu1oii0.

"The Assault Weapons Ban Didn't Work. A New Version Won't, Either." *Los Angeles Times*, March 1, 2018. https://www.latimes.com/opinion /op-ed/la-oe-stokes-assault-weapon-ban-20180301-story.htmlv.

Bilton, Ricardo. "25 Trump Voters from Alabama + 25 Clinton Voters from San Francisco = 1 Surprisingly Good Facebook Group." Nieman Lab, March 16, 2017. https://www.niemanlab.org/2017/03/50 -trump-voters-from-alabama-50-clinton-voters-from-san-francisco -1-surprisingly-good-facebook-group/.

Ciobanu, Madalina. "Spaceship Media Is Using 'Dialogue Journalism' to Enable Productive Conversations between Communities at Odds."

Further Reading

Journalism.co.uk, January 9, 2018. https://www.journalism.co.uk/news /spaceship-media-is-using-dialogue-journalism-to-enable-productive -conversations-between-communities-at-odds/s2/a715850/.

Cohn, D'Vera, Paul Taylor, Mark Hugo Lopez, Catherine A. Gallagher, Kim Parker, and Kevin T. Maass. "Gun Homicide Rate Down 49% Since 1993 Peak; Public Unaware." Pew Research Center's Social & Demographic Trends Project, May 7, 2013. https://www .pewsocialtrends.org/2013/05/07/gun-homicide-rate-down-49-since -1993-peak-public-unaware/?fbclid=IwAR0KjF256D0_bPMkx8Yi dAyRmG9dM396XcOqkIYOGRoranBetcYbhjqEfYs.

Cook, Philip J., and Kristin A. Goss. "The Gun Debate: What Everyone Needs to Know." Amazon. https://www.amazon.com/Gun-Debate -Everyone-Needs-Know®/dp/019933899X?fbclid=IwAR2KwWyto3 MLw3oQhGo-cuReJcBfreA6ae-kxSYO_GtD95aWen5_h37G84k.

Costello, Amy. "Hey, America: Let's Talk About What Divides Us." Nonprofit Quarterly, November 16, 2018. https://nonprofitquarterly .org/hey-america-lets-talk-about-what-divides-us/.

"Fatal Injury Reports, National, Regional and State, 1981–2018." WISQARS. Centers for Disease Control and Prevention. https://web appa.cdc.gov/sasweb/ncipc/mortrate.html?fbclid=IwAR2_IlYAd8u TOPA5_WsGb1NYnBawqSd8bJLWiney668wr7YUzkS1dZTWpbY.

Gius, Mark. "Concealed Carry Laws and Assault Weapons Bans Do Not Have a Significant Effect on the Gun-Related Murder Rate at the State Level." LSE US Centre, January 16, 2014. https://blogs.lse.ac.uk /usappblog/2014/01/16/concealed-carry-laws-and-assault-weapons -bans-do-not-have-a-significant-effect-on-the-gun-related-murder -rate-at-the-state-level/?fbclid=IwAR0eavh2MVr1mqFOzqDVBGbn U8bOs1P4j4J8YD0nyqplKjyngNRIFLR9AiY.

Further Reading

———. "The Effects of State and Federal Gun Control Laws on School Shootings." Philadelphia: Taylor & Francis, April 19, 2017. https://www.tandfonline.com/doi/abs/10.1080/13504851.2017.1319555?fbclid=IwAR3ARmZUGqI7CA4BfgGO8qRzwCpbabbnKLFHF57Z9aLsJthcOchfGPry6s&scroll=top&needAccess=true&journalCode=rael20.

"Guns, An American Conversation." Spaceship Media. Accessed February 21, 2020. https://spaceshipmedia.org/projects/guns-an-american-conversation/.

"HR 3355—Violent Crime Control and Law Enforcement Act of 1994." Congress.gov. https://www.congress.gov/bill/103rd-congress/house-bill/3355/text?fbclid=IwAR2Z03wzr6GoYuuCich9fX1xoBh8YL6nHVXzfFKAYJkzzrKhEQ54XGtIjUc.

"Introduction." Spaceship Media. Accessed February 20, 2020. https://spaceshipmedia.org/toolkit/introduction/#book-download-hdr.

"It's Time to Bring Back the Assault Weapons Band, Gun Violence Experts Say." *Washington Post*, February 15, 2018. https://www.washingtonpost.com/news/wonk/wp/2018/02/15/its-time-to-bring-back-the-assault-weapons-ban-gun-violence-experts-say/?fbclid=IwAR0-70jcn_F6YYoPnOS-9jNtFq3yt6i7x2N_zGXnmRwPnwtmNFD7VH5yGR8.

Kolbert, Elizabeth. "Why Facts Don't Change Our Minds." *New Yorker*, July 9, 2019. https://www.newyorker.com/magazine/2017/02/27/why-facts-dont-change-our-minds.

Koper, Christopher S., Daniel J. Woods, and Jeffrey A. Roth. "An Updated Assessment of the Federal Assault Weapons Ban: Impacts on Gun Markets and Gun Violence, 1994–2003," June 2004. https://www.ncjrs.gov/pdffiles1/nij/grants/204431.pdf?fbclid=IwAR2ygZ5_hlo5Xm4aDT8bBtmm1LVTyfcOWU-mTDysWkucdW5kZCnQlbAS_Yw.

Further Reading

Montgomery, Ben, Kelley Benham French, and Thomas French. "21 Americans with Opposing Views on Guns Sat Down to Talk to Each Other. Here's What They Discovered." *Time*, June 28, 2018. https://time.com/longform/both-sides-gun-control/.

Murphy, Sherry L., Jiaquan Xu, Kenneth D. Kochanek, Sally C. Curtin, and Elizabeth Arias. "Deaths: Final Data for 2015." *National Vital Statistics Reports* 66, no. 6 (November 27, 2017). https://www.cdc.gov/nchs/data/nvsr/nvsr66/nvsr66_06.pdf?fbclid=IwAR0XBOWjIHKQX X4C6QPqgc7HfG4VDOq0XwGvUcCx1Tvmlapex8jzfxY3Wmg.

Murray, Caroline, and Natalie Jomini Stroud. "Making Strangers Less Strange." Center for Media Engagement, November 2018. https://mediaengagement.org/research/making-strangers-less-strange/.

Pearlman, Eve. "How to Lead a Conversation Between People Who Disagree." TED, January 2019. https://www.ted.com/talks/eve_pearlman_how_to_lead_a_conversation_between_people_who_disagree?nolanguage=en).

Plumer, Brad. "Everything You Need to Know About the Assault Weapons Ban, in One Post." *Washington Post*, December 17, 2012.

Ripley, Amanda. "Complicating the Narratives." *Solutions Journalism*, June 27, 2018. https://thewholestory.solutionsjournalism.org/complicating-the-narratives-b91ea06ddf63.

Rosenfeld, Richard, Shytierra Gaston, Howard Spivak, and Seri Irazola. "Assessing and Responding to the Recent Homicide Rise in the United States." National Institute of Justice, November 2017. https://www.ncjrs.gov/pdffiles1/nij/251067.pdf?fbclid=IwAR2LmBhEDRkxpnI32 eWsoVYwxeuRRYXca4mj9oeh72ypynqXqIQfu-spFoM.

Further Reading

Schaffer, Jan. "Deepening Engagement: Reciprocity Could Be Key for Journalists." Medium.com, Disruptive Journalism Educators Network, June 30, 2016. https://medium.com/teaching-media-entrepreneurship /deepening-engagement-c19ae95de97b.

Smart, Rosanna. "Effects of Bans on the Sale of Assault Weapons and High-Capacity Magazines on Mass Shootings." Rand, March 2, 2018. https://www.rand.org/research/gun-policy/analysis/ban-assault -weapons/mass-shootings.html?fbclid=IwAR1DwtLGVNMsq-i06C _vXoo8bK1EwnPCHK5JpJhcEBBjVOwBz0hKLUiDa5A.

Tsai, Diane, Francesca Trianni, and Susanna Schrobsdorff. "These 21 Americans Came Together to Discuss Gun Control." *Time*, April 4, 2018. https://time.com/5226590/guns-conversation-america/.

Notes

Chapter 1

1. Stephen Koff, "Should the AR-15 and Other Semi-Automatic Weapons Be Regulated? 'Guns, An American Conversation,'" AL, April 18, 2018, https://www.al.com/news/2018/04/should_the_ar-15_and_other _sem.html.

2. "About Us," Advance Local, https://www.advancelocal.com/about-us/.

3. "Local Connections. National Impact," Advance Local, https://www .advancelocal.com/.

4. "About Us." Spaceship Media, https://spaceshipmedia.org/about/.

5. Eve Pearlman, "How to Lead a Conversation Between People Who Disagree," TED, January 2019, https://www.ted.com/talks/eve_pearlman _how_to_lead_a_conversation_between_people_who_disagree/trans cript?language=en#t-120587.

6. Jeremy Hay and Eve Pearlman, "As Conversation Winds Down, Women from Alabama and California Discuss Race, Other Chal-

Notes

lenges," AL, January 15, 2017, https://www.al.com/news/birmingham /2017/01/as_conversation_winds_down_wom.html.

7. "The Role of Guns in American Life," Essential Partners, https:// whatisessential.org/topic/guns.

8. *United States v. Miller*, Cornell Law School, https://www.law.cornell.edu /supct/search/display.html?terms=United States V Miller&url=/supct /html/historics/USSC_CR_0307_0174_ZS.html.

9. *District of Columbia v. Heller*, 554 US 570 (2008), Justia Law, https:// supreme.justia.com/cases/federal/us/554/570/.

10. *McDonald v. Chicago*, 561 US 742 (2010), Justia Law, https://supreme .justia.com/cases/federal/us/561/742/.

11. *National Rifle Association of America Incorporated v. McCraw*, Bloomberg Law, https://www.bloomberglaw.com/public/desktop/document /Natl_Rifle_Assn_of_America_Inc_v_McCraw_719_F3d_338_5th _Cir_2013_?1522352432.

12. Ibid.

13. *Jackson v. City and County of San Francisco*, Findlaw, https://caselaw .findlaw.com/us-9th-circuit/1661065.html.

14. Fred Barbash and Meagan Flynn, "Does the Second Amendment Really Protect Assault Weapons? Four Courts Have Said No," *Washington Post*, February 22, 2018, https://www.washingtonpost.com/news /morning-mix/wp/2018/02/22/does-the-second-amendment-really -protect-assault-weapons-four-courts-have-said-no/.

15. Stephen Koff, https://connect.al.com/staff/skoff/posts.html.

16. "Mission & Story," March for Our Lives, https://marchforourlives .com/mission-story/.

17. Sonam Sheth, "'Fight for Your Lives Before It's Someone Else's Job': Parkland Student Emma Gonzalez Sends a Powerful Message at the

Notes

'March for Our Lives' Rally," *Business Insider*, March 24, 2018, https://
www.businessinsider.com/emma-gonzalez-six-minutes-speech
-march-for-our-lives-rally-2018-3.

18. "March for Our Lives Highlights: Students Protesting Guns Say
    'Enough Is Enough,'" *New York Times*, March 24, 2018, https://www
    .nytimes.com/2018/03/24/us/march-for-our-lives.html.

19. David Weigel, "NRA Goes on the Offensive After Parkland Shoot-
    ing, Assailing Media and Calling for More Armed School Security,"
    Washington Post, February 23, 2018, https://www.washingtonpost
    .com/news/post-nation/wp/2018/02/22/after-silence-on-parkland
    -nra-pushes-back-against-law-enforcement-the-media-and-gun
    -control-advocates/.

20. Diane Tsai, Francesca Trianni, and Susanna Schrobsdorff, "These 21
    Americans Came Together to Discuss Gun Control," *Time*, April 4,
    2018, https://time.com/5226590/guns-conversation-america/.

21. Ibid.

Chapter 2

1. "Dialogue Journalism, the Method," Spaceship Media, https://docs
   .google.com/document/d/1bX3orMFcRQ5M-oX9rg7bMLtJeG
   i4igqD-nM7HN4UNAk/edit.

2. Adriana Garcia, Cailley LaPara, and Eve Pearlman, "Dialogue Journalism Toolkit," Spaceship Media, https://spaceshipmedia.org/wp
   -content/uploads/2019/06/toolkit-526.pdf.

3. "Dialogue Journalism, the Method."

4. Jeff Daniels, "Definition of What's Actually an 'Assault Weapon' Is a
   Highly Contentious Issue," CNBC, February 27, 2018, https://www
   .cnbc.com/2018/02/21/definition-of-whats-an-assault-weapon-is-a
   -very-contentious-issue.html.

Notes

5. "HR 3355—Violent Crime Control and Law Enforcement Act of 1994," Congress.gov, https://www.congress.gov/bill/103rd-congress/house-bill/3355/text.

6. "Bullet Button Assault Weapon," State of California, Department of Justice, Office of the Attorney General, July 1, 2018, https://oag.ca.gov/firearms/bullet-button-assault-weapon.

7. "The Writer's Guide to Firearms & Ammunition," Firearms Industry Association, http://www3.nssf.org/share/PDF/WritersGuide2017.pdf.

8. "Assault Weapons vs. Semi Automatic Guns," Buckeye Firearms Association, https://www.buckeyefirearms.org/assault-weapons-vs-semi-automatic-guns.

9. Joshua Gillin, "The Difference Between Automatic and Semi-Automatic Weapons," Politifact, October 2, 2017, https://www.politifact.com/truth-o-meter/article/2017/oct/02/difference-between-automatic-and-semi-automatic-we/.

10. Tom Kehoe, "How Many Rounds Does a Semi-Automatic Rifle Fire per Minute?" Quora, June 21, 2016, https://www.quora.com/How-many-rounds-does-a-semi-automatic-rifle-fire-per-minute.

11. Eric Limer, "Vegas Shooter Had 'Bump Stocks' to Give Rifles to Full-Auto Firing Rates," *Popular Mechanics*, February 20, 2018, https://www.popularmechanics.com/technology/news/a28479/vegas-shooter-bump-stock/.

12. Larry Buchanan, Evan Grothjan, Jon Huang, Yuliya Parshina-Kottas, Adam Pearce, and Karen Yourish, "What Is a Bump Stock and How Does It Work?" *New York Times*, October 4, 2017, https://www.nytimes.com/interactive/2017/10/04/us/bump-stock-las-vegas-gun.html.

13. "NRA's Wayne LaPierre and Chris Cox Issue Joint Statement," NRA, https://home.nra.org/joint-statement.

Notes

14. "Department of Justice Submits Notice of Proposed Regulation Banning Bump Stocks," US Department of Justice, March 10, 2018, https://www.justice.gov/opa/pr/department-justice-submits-notice-proposed-regulation-banning-bump-stocks.

15. Jon Schuppe, "America's Rifle: Why So Many People Love the AR-15," NBC News, December 27, 2017, https://www.nbcnews.com/news/us-news/america-s-rifle-why-so-many-people-love-ar-15-n831171.

16. "4 Basic Questions About the AR-15," *Washington Post*, February 16, 2018, https://www.washingtonpost.com/news/checkpoint/wp/2018/02/15/4-basic-questions-about-the-ar-15/.

17. Stephen Koff, https://connect.al.com/staff/skoff/posts.html.

Chapter 3

1. Stephen Koff, AL, https://connect.al.com/staff/skoff/posts.html.

2. "Concealed Carry Reciprocity Agreements," Ohio attorney general Dave Yost, https://www.ohioattorneygeneral.gov/Law-Enforcement/Concealed-Carry/Concealed-Carry-Reciprocity-Agreements.

3. "Concealed Carry Reciprocity Is on the Move: Your Lawmakers Need to Hear from You NOW!" NRA, November 27, 2017, https://www.nraila.org/articles/20171127/concealed-carry-reciprocity-is-on-the-move-your-lawmakers-need-to-hear-from-you-now.

4. "HR 38—Concealed Carry Reciprocity Act of 2017," Congress.gov, https://www.congress.gov/bill/115th-congress/house-bill/38?q={"search":["concealed+carry+reciprocity+act"]}.

5. John Deike, "17-Year-Old Gunned down on Cleveland's East Side," *Cleveland 19 News*, August 12, 2018, https://www.cleveland19.com/story/37946326/17-year-old-boy-shot-in-the-head-on-clevelands-east-side/?fbclid=IwAR1sRKtmiouy6ecTwSfnrMRb26W6vCP2zjcn5lpB5orQMDaOXSVogxfzZ7Q.

Notes

6. "2018, United States All Injury Deaths and Rates per 100,000," Centers for Disease Control and Prevention, https://webappa.cdc.gov/cgi -bin/broker.exe.

7. Suzanne Lea, "'Death by Legal Intervention' by the Numbers," Psychology Benefits Society, July 2, 2015, https://psychologybenefits .org/2015/07/02/police-shootings-data/?fbclid=IwAR3bEbdnMS3z 10f5aRrtu0NXNYigJSXLSDjWuNkslqxtMwfQtRJLurKbvjM.

8. Richard Rosenfeld, Shytierra Gaston, Howard Spivak, and Seri Irazola, "Assessing and Responding to the Recent Homicide Rise in the United States," National Institute of Justice, November 2017, https:// www.ncjrs.gov/pdffiles1/nij/251067.pdf?fbclid=IwAR2uUzmv6k _FMZDji4ijHAO4gjJgaDvLbnz33kc9NrXZ6MaUh-BM4dDfylI.

9. D'Vera Cohn, Paul Taylor, Mark Hugo Lopez, Catherine A. Gallagher, Kim Parker, and Kevin T. Maass, "Gun Homicide Rate Down 49% Since 1993 Peak; Public Unaware," Pew Research Center's Social & Demographic Trends Project, December 31, 2019, https://www .pewsocialtrends.org/2013/05/07/gun-homicide-rate-down-49-since -1993-peak-public-unaware/?fbclid=IwAR31OmsOjgHnvWvfzdiO UWR-Auot3X5qELf2CfgKhLyCNH1PfpZUjMFcJp8.

10. Sherry L. Murphy, Jiaquan Xu, Kenneth D. Kochanek, Sally C. Curtin, and Elizabeth Arias, "Deaths: Final Data for 2015," *National Vital Statistics Reports* 66, no. 6 (November 27, 2017), https://www .cdc.gov/nchs/data/nvsr/nvsr66/nvsr66_06.pdf?fbclid=IwAR3dhN -Ji2uyVK5Ya4_M1jwO4Cd3uEmFpJkJbpjqB7-Zd9z2e0k3rJLLdn0.

Chapter 4

1. Christopher S. Koper, Daniel J. Woods, and Jeffrey A. Roth, "An Updated Assessment of the Federal Assault Weapons Ban: Impacts on Gun Markets and Gun Violence, 1994–2003," June 2004, https:// www.ncjrs.gov/pdffiles1/nij/grants/204431.pdf?fbclid=IwAR2ygZ5 _hlo5Xm4aDT8bBtmm1LVTyfcOWU-mTDysWkucdW5kZCn QlbAS_Yw.

Notes

2. Robert Farley, "Did the 1994 Assault Weapons Ban Work?" FactCheck .org, February 1, 2013, https://www.factcheck.org/2013/02/did-the -1994-assault-weapons-ban-work/?fbclid=IwAR2eDXlpRN3hursda pORnUP7Nd1XaUZpzG-JXVAY_psxTF3zBBWWZsSgjNY.

3. "Gun Violence Archive," Gun Violence Archive, https://www.gun violencearchive.org/?fbclid=IwAR28FZsTUosBaQPGRmi_jzA6O-QdnUHSK484dXzm4d88U3rTp4Kf0h1PuDL8.

4. "General Methodology," Gun Violence Archive, https://www.gunvio lencearchive.org/methodology?fbclid=IwAR1wxWQF-YomBPGor dlMOHdn042bRBJp4CbuIz8Vzomqpg9TxIFnFgBTlvs.

5. Rosanna Smart, "Mass Shootings: Definitions and Trends," Rand, March 2, 2018, https://www.rand.org/research/gun-policy/analysis /essays/mass-shootings.html.

6. "It's Time to Bring Back the Assault Weapons Ban, Gun Violence Experts Say," *Washington Post*, February 15, 2018, https://www .washingtonpost.com/news/wonk/wp/2018/02/15/its-time-to-bring-back-the-assault-weapons-ban-gun-violence-experts-say /?fbclid=IwAR0-70jcn_F6YYoPnOS-9jNtFq3yt6i7x2N_zGXnmRw PnwtmNFD7VH5yGR8.

7. "The Assault Weapons Ban Didn't Work. A New Version Won't, Either," *Los Angeles Times*, March 1, 2018, https://www.latimes.com /opinion/op-ed/la-oe-stokes-assault-weapon-ban20180301-story .htmlv.

8. Rosanna Smart, "Effects of Bans on the Sale of Assault Weapons and High-Capacity Magazines on Mass Shootings," Rand, March 2, 2018, https://www.rand.org/research/gun-policy/analysis/ban-assault -weapons/mass-shootings.html?fbclid=IwAR1DwtLGVNMsq -i06C_vXoo8bK1EwnPCHK5JpJhcEBBjVOwBz0hKLUiDa5A.

9. Mark Gius, "The Effects of State and Federal Gun Control Laws on School Shootings" (Philadelphia: Taylor & Francis), April 19, 2017, https://www.tandfonline.com/doi/abs/10.1080/13504851.2017

Notes

.1319555?fbclid=IwAR3ARmZUGqI7CA4BfgGO8qRzwC
pbabbnKLFHF57Z9aLsJthcOchfGPry6s&scroll=top&needAccess
=true&journalCode=rael20.

10. Mark Gius, "Concealed Carry Laws and Assault Weapons Bans Do
    Not Have a Significant Effect on the Gun-Related Murder Rate at
    the State Level," LSE US Centre, January 16, 2014, https://blogs
    .lse.ac.uk/usappblog/2014/01/16/concealed-carry-laws-and-assault
    -weapons-bans-do-not-have-a-significant-effect-on-the-gun-related
    -murder-rate-at-the-state-level/?fbclid=IwAR0eavh2MVr1mqFOzq
    DVBGbnU8bOs1P4j4J8YD0nyqplKjyngNRIFLR9AiY.

Additional Resources

1. Ruth Igielnik and Anna Brown, "Americans' Views on Guns and Gun
   Ownership: 8 Key Findings," Pew Research Center, June 22, 2017,
   https://www.pewresearch.org/fact-tank/2017/06/22/key-takeaways
   -on-americans-views-of-guns-and-gun-ownership/?fbclid=IwAR
   2QPOTD1ETlXAdi7uAxkYAIJaPAF-6nbb42DUuOvZT-SXe2Ru
   GHXLMuv2A.

2. Pew Research Center, https://www.pewresearch.org/?fbclid=IwAR2
   RT6Z5y5ANoNWMyNyYo4ULQDNLgSeoW48HlxEjM3jAwW3
   1zVEXuLD7oRo.

3. Kim Parker, Juliana Menasce Horowitz, Ruth Igielnik, J. Baxter
   Oliphant, and Anna Brown, "America's Complex Relationship with
   Guns," Pew Research Center's Social & Demographic Trends Pro-
   ject, June 22, 2017, https://www.pewsocialtrends.org/2017/06/22/the
   -demographics-of-gun-ownership/?fbclid=IwAR3PrK0msWQKp7
   CcWCO3Jse3UWBp1iRWR14JSH9qHXn82Qz7m3d95Bse4AA.

4. "FAQ," US Census Bureau, https://www.census.gov/topics/popula
   tion/hispanic-origin/about/faq.html?fbclid=IwAR23U3-u8Az5
   hEsicjOFhT8IuTIFoosGCpxGMwe9c7_aX5qKdgp8M8MU4U4.

5. Parker, Horowitz, Igielnik, Oliphant, and Brown, "America's Complex
   Relationship with Guns."

6. Ibid.

7. "Amid Rising Gun Violence, Accidental Shootings Have Plummeted. Why?" *Los Angeles Times*; Parker, Horowitz, Igielnik, Oliphant, and Brown, "America's Complex Relationship with Guns."

8. Ibid.

9. D'Vera Cohn, Paul Taylor, Mark Hugo Lopez, Catherine A. Gallagher, Kim Parker, and Kevin T. Maass, "Gun Homicide Rate Down 49% Since 1993 Peak; Public Unaware," Pew Research Center's Social & Demographic Trends Project, December 31, 2019, https://www.pewsocialtrends.org/2013/05/07/gun-homicide-rate-down-49-since-1993-peak-public-unaware/.

Index

163

Index

Index

Index

Index

Index

Index

Index

Index

About the Author

Launched after the 2016 election with a mission to reduce polarization, build communities, and restore trust in journalism, **Spaceship Media** has quickly become a leader in engaging communities around difficult issues and supporting civil, fact-based conversations. Spaceship Media's Dialogue Journalism method reconceptualizes the information and reporting process and puts the divided communities Spaceship and their journalistic partners serve at the heart of their practice. Spaceship has conceptualized and created conversations about such polarizing issues as immigration, income disparity, gun safety, race, education, and national politics. With their approach to moderating difficult conversations and their style of reporting directly for communities, they have built a track record of success. Spaceship Media's collaborators include Advance Local, *Time*, Essential Partners, Minnesota Public Radio/American Public Media, Univision, the *Seattle Times*, Bay Area News Group, and Southern California News Group.